Tours with Children and Teens

A Handbook for Docents and Guides

Betsy Vourlekis
Smithsonian National Museum of Asian Art Freer Gallery of Art and Arthur M. Sackler Gallery

Jan Thorman
The Walters Art Museum

Lindsay McAuliffe
Smithsonian National Museum of Asian Art Freer Gallery of Art and Arthur M. Sackler Gallery

A Publication of the
National Docent Symposium Council
www.nationaldocents.org

Tours with Children and Teens

Copyright 2022 Betsy Vourlekis, Jan Thorman, Lindsay McAuliffe

1. EDU029100 Education / Teaching / Methods & Strategies
2. EDU057000 Education / Arts in Education
3. ART059000 Art / Museum Studies

ISBN: 9798886360073

The kaleidoscope was designed by Jan Wallake, Toledo Art Museum, Toledo, Ohio.

For information about the National Docent Symposium Council and for ordering Tours with Children and Teens, please visit www.nationaldocents.org.

Printed by Authority Publishing, Gold River, California

Contents

Introduction

A visit to a museum is "an intense, hands-on, beautiful assault on the senses that breathes life into art, history, science, culture etc., in a way that is nearly impossible to replicate in a classroom, through a textbook, or via the internet."

Anthony Pennay
https://museumquestions.com/2015/04/14/what-management-lessons-from-teaching-transfer-to-the-museum/

In 2017, the National Docent Symposium Council published *The Docent Handbook 2,* the second edition of the original *Docent Handbook* published in 2001. Feedback on the 2017 *Handbook* indicated that it is a useful resource for docents and guides, and that more is needed specifically on tours for our younger visitors. This new publication builds on *The Docent Handbook 2,* which provides fundamental information for all docents/guides about successfully touring and guiding groups of any age. Docents not yet familiar with the foundation information contained in *Handbook 2* may want to refer to that book first or in tandem with this one.

Tours with Children and Teens enhances and deepens information and guidance for touring with children pre-K through high school, home schoolers and multi-aged groups, and those with special needs. It provides practical help and suggestions, based on research, and offers extensive examples from a variety of museums. Museums are moving rapidly forward with a digital presence, and virtual tours for children and teens are a reality. We offer a final chapter discussing opportunities and challenges for these tours and insights based on what is still very much a developing process. The approaches presented throughout the handbook are equally relevant for in-person and virtual tours. We hope *Tours with Children and Teens* will inspire confidence and enjoyment for our important work with young visitors.

Why tours for youth matter

Pre-school and school-aged youth may be the most important visitors to museums and other cultural institutions. A positive experience on a school tour can encourage families to visit again and help lay the groundwork for adult museum enthusiasts. School tours give us the opportunity to establish a connection with our next generation, the future stewards of the museum. A successful tour can instill a desire in students to return with friends and family. By valuing their observations and empowering their voices, we make children and teens feel welcome in the museum.

Museum visits provide rich visual reinforcement for school curriculum and learning objectives. Even a brief opportunity to look and wonder can widen horizons for young people, expose them to the beliefs and cultures of diverse communities, and demonstrate the vast range of human talent and the creation of beauty.

Young people are passionate about the struggles to achieve greater social justice and human rights for all. They care about fairness for themselves and for others. These struggles and needed actions involve our museums–in their operations and priorities, the exhibitions they craft, and the audiences they seek to engage. Our tours create opportunities to explore and validate this mission, so critical for our pluralistic democracy, with the groups that will shape our future. As docents and guides, we can design tours that model tolerance, understanding and respect for diverse cultures, as well as expose younger audiences to the richness of global creative expression.

Museum visits, thoughtfully crafted with questions, exercises and age-appropriate information, are ideally suited to help prepare young visitors with the general life skills essential for adult functioning in the future. Skills of empathy and perspective-taking, close observation and visual literacy–the ability to understand how meaning is made in images–critical thinking, communication, creativity and global understanding are modeled and practiced on well-designed tours.

Teachers value museum field trips to expand and illustrate curriculum in many areas–social studies, history, science, math, reading and writing, art and art appreciation, religious studies and more. Viewing and interacting with museum objects and displays afford students an immediate exposure, perhaps even a hands-on encounter, with a reality only described in books or viewed from pictures and digital screens. Carefully designed tours offer young people practice in critical inquiry and observational skills along with deepening content understanding. Above all, a museum visit is an opportunity for young visitors to find their own personal relevance in what they view.

Touring with children and teens gives docents and guides the satisfaction of both learning and sharing. Young visitors bring amazement, curiosity, imagination, and sharp eyes, burnishing our familiar objects with freshness and new insights and understanding. Visitors share their own life experiences and are curious about ours. Visitors ask "Why are we docents? Have we visited or seen where this object came from? What nationality is our name? Do we paint? Make ceramics? Garden? Why?" Exchanges with young people are an always variable, often funny, educational, and deeply satisfying aspect of what we do.

Museums and their interactions with youth are becoming two-way streets. Many museums have been transitioning from *collection*-centered to *people*-centered organizations. One way that is done successfully is by cultivating empathy and deep listening for meaningful exchanges with our diverse communities, including young people. Museums of all types need to reflect and honor the realities, passions, and commitments of their multiple publics if they are to thrive. What does this mean? Instead of just focusing on the information and insights *we* want to impart, we encourage visitors to bring their own enthusiasm, interests, and insights. One of the purposes of this handbook is to offer tools and approaches for how to do this with children and teens.

Using this handbook

Tours with Children and Teens is best used in conjunction with *The Docent Handbook 2*, which provides much useful information about being a

docent/guide*, tour planning, and touring with different audiences. This handbook includes detailed information and principles about tours for younger visitors that are derived from age-specific information about the youngest to oldest school visitors, as well as children with special needs. It considers tough topics that may arise during tours, all aspects of tour management, and provides resources where you can learn more. We leave space for you to add your own notes and experiences to this handbook to make it even more useful for your personal practice.

Chapter One, "Basics," discusses seven key ideas that underlie successful touring with younger audiences. "Getting Started" is a step-by-step guide to planning tours, emphasizing the process of communicating and collaborating with teachers and other adults. There are three "audiences" chapters starting with our youngest visitors, continuing in Chapter Four, which discusses teens, and Chapter Five, home schoolers, after-school groups, and multi-aged groups.

For each age group, we present a series of specific, research-based points of developmentally relevant information. Each is followed by a "Therefore" statement that fleshes out implications for successful tour strategies. These are illustrated with examples from different museum settings. Boxes throughout present specific tour examples. Chapter Six focuses on youth with special needs. We provide background information that explains the importance of an array of considerations and techniques–many of which are basic to any tour, but often crucial for successful touring with uniquely challenged audience members.

Chapter Seven, "Candid Conversations," offers best-practice ideas and strategies to create positive engagement with youth around issues that may generate controversy and awkwardness. Chapter Eight considers behaviors that arise during tours that can be challenging for docents. It explains why some behaviors occur and discusses helpful and constructive approaches for dealing with infrequent occurrences. We provide a range of management strategies and techniques. The final chapter, "Live Virtual Tours," is a look at providing live tours from a distance. Docent/guide practice will continue to evolve and change as schools adapt to combinations of remote and in-class learning. Technology will improve and shift as well. Many of the touring techniques discussed throughout this handbook apply equally to virtual tours. We consider this an early look at some basic information for virtual touring.

At the end of this handbook, we include a resource/ reference list as a guide for learning more. Resources are also available from the National Docent Symposium Council website, nationaldocents.org, and private Facebook group, National Docents Forum.

*We include here the dual term docent/guide, recognizing that different museums may use one or the other. We made the editorial decision not to repeat the dual indicator in every instance.

YOUR PERSONAL NOTES

1 Basics

As a docent, you have an understanding of your role, subject expertise in your museum's collection, and general skills for tour planning and dealing with diverse audiences. A refresher read through *The Docent Handbook 2*'s first chapter, "Foundations," will remind you of the "basics" for any docent. Here we emphasize and expand on a set of basics for tours with younger visitors, whether coming from schools, home schooled, or with family and other adults.

Here are seven basic guiding principles: more about each later.

- Enjoy your visitors
- Know your subject
- Put the needs of the learners first
- Engage children and teens through meaningful discussion and activities
- Plan your tour with thought and care
- Be flexible
- Enjoy yourself

Enjoy and value your visitors

The most basic, bedrock tenet for working with children and teens is that we tour with respect and enthusiasm. Kids of all ages pose challenges and opportunities that are different from those of adults. As with any visitor to the museum, we need to let our student visitors know we are happy they have come and are excited to share and learn with them. Later we talk about strategies for handling challenging behaviors while maintaining a positive attitude and modeling respect. Many docents prefer tours with young people for the fun, spontaneity, and unique responses and insights they bring.

Know your subject

Throughout this handbook we emphasize that lecturing kids on a tour is not a successful strategy. Yet even the youngest visitors come to the museum to learn about what they are seeing. Providing useful, age-appropriate information connected to the responses and interests of young visitors requires deep knowledge about the objects and artifacts and their context. You will not be able to "teach" all that you know, of course. You convey what is relevant to the discussions and process of the tour, drawing from your knowledge base. The "teaching tension" between providing useful content (your knowledge of the objects and their context) and successfully keeping the interest and involvement of our visitors can be resolved by letting content come from the curiosity, responses, and actions of the young visitors themselves. A successful tour connects information with engaging activities, discussions, and questions, and will be fun.

Put the needs of learners first

Successful tours for children and teens start with the fundamental understanding that the tour is an experience, not a lecture. Our visitors come to learn, and content matters. However, what makes the museum visit engaging and exciting for them and the content memorable, are their own questions, discoveries, and connections. For this to happen, we prioritize strategies that engage young visitors of different ages. The expression, "Be the guide on the side, not the sage on the stage" captures this basic principle.

Engage with children and teens through meaningful discussion and activities

This is the "how to" for putting the learner first. Getting your audience fully engaged, not simply present and listening, is accomplished through asking for their thoughts and ideas and providing opportunities for active exploration and discovery. Throughout the handbook, we explore why and how to do this successfully with each age group. We provide examples of questions, prompts and routines to tap curiosity and generate thinking and discussion. We describe techniques for sharing and comparing ideas in the tour group and samples of tour activities. Here we discuss successful ways to engage your audience that are illustrated throughout the rest of the handbook. Remember, too, much of what we present works for both virtual and in-person tours.

Ask useful questions

An important goal of your museum tour is to develop self-confident visitors who know how to think and feel for themselves. Our questions can help equip students to live thoughtfully in a visual world and talk about visual objects. This is often called *visual literacy*. We do this by asking questions that open debate or dialogue and inquire about the unknown, rather than testing knowledge. We move from simple to more complex questions, from questions that ask for description *(What do you see here?)* to interpretation *(What do you notice that makes you say that?)* to ones that ask for analysis and reflection *(How do the parts of the piece interact? What values/emotions come into play for you as you look? How did the arrival of Europeans affect Native Peoples' traditional hunting practices? What is the continuing legacy of the environmental impact of hydraulic mining?)* We ask questions that probe for personal meaning in response to what is viewed and questions that invite putting oneself in others' shoes.

Open-ended questions have multiple appropriate answers. They do not have yes or no answers, nor do they ask students to recall information.

- Touring an exhibit showing the daily life of long-ago people, you might ask, *What do you think is the most useful tool? What is the least?*
- Looking at a contemporary painting called "Untitled," you ask, *What title would you give this painting? What do you see/feel/experience that led you to choose that title? Why do you think the artist chose to call it Untitled?*

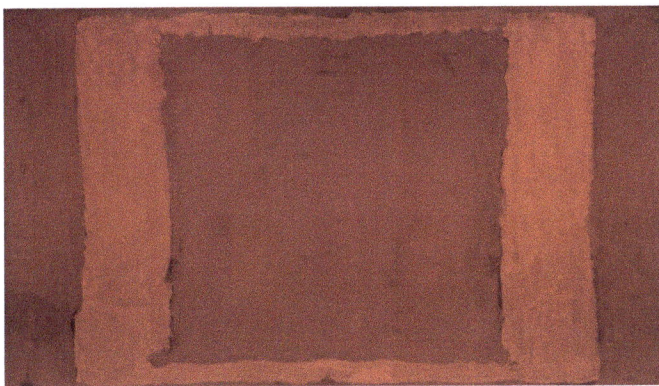

Mark Rothko, "Untitled," From the Seagram Murals Series, 1959, National Gallery of Art, © 1998 Kate Rothko Prizel & Christopher Rothko / Artists Rights Society (ARS), New York

- For a tour highlighting how medieval artists evoked the idea of God, looking at an image of Mary with baby Jesus, you might ask, *What do you see that might tell you something about the relationship between these two figures? How do the colors/textures/shapes/lines the artist used affect your feelings about the painting?*

As students reply to questions, paraphrase their replies, link them to make their interaction obvious, and show how listening and responding to others enriches the conversation and the examination of an object or work.

Descriptive questions encourage students to develop their observational skills. For this image we might ask:

- *How would you describe the figures in this work?*
- *How would you describe the clothes the boy is wearing?*
- *If you could touch the dog, how do you think it might feel? What do you see that makes you say that?*
- *What colors do you see in this work?*
- *Where do you think the boy and dog are? What do you see that makes you say that?*

Sofonisba Anguissola, "Portrait of Marquess Massimiliano Stampa," 1557, oil on canvas. Acquired by Henry Walters, 1927, acc. no. 37.1016. Photo courtesy of The Walters Art Museum, Baltimore

Interpretive questions help students explore the meaning of artworks. After the students have looked carefully at a work, guided by descriptive questions, you can ask them to offer opinions that can be supported by what they see.

- *How do you think the boy feels? What do you see that makes you say that?*
- *How do you think it would feel to wear clothes like what we see here?*
- *How do you think your feelings about the painting might be affected by a different color background—maybe red instead of green? Or what color would you choose?*
- *Why do you think the artist included the dog?*
- *Why do you think the artist used the same colors for the dog and the base of the column the boy is leaning on?*
- *Why do you think the artist filled the whole painting top to bottom with the boy? How do you think your feelings about the painting would change if the artist had shown him in a big room with lots of space around him?*
- *If you were going to introduce the boy to your friends, what would you say about him?*
- *If you were going to give him a social media handle, something with a hashtag, what would it be? Why?*

A **concluding question** at the end of the tour provides an opportunity for review and recall and for visitors to cement a final personal link with what they have seen and experienced. A simple *What object did you like best?* or *What will you most remember?* and *Why?* will do this. For older visitors, you might ask *Of the works you looked at today, which one can you most relate to? and Why? or Which felt most relevant to our world today? or Which object was most familiar/unfamiliar?*

Employ slow looking
Provide prompts that encourage young visitors to look carefully and for a significant amount of time (a minute or two) at an artifact or object or one of its parts. Educator Shari Tishman defines slow looking as "taking the time to carefully observe more than meets the eye at first glance." Encouraging patient attention to details, called "immersive viewing," allows for discovery of more meaning and promotes critical thinking. It moves viewers beyond first impressions, allowing for a more complex understanding. The section on artful thinking routines and activities, below, is an application of this general approach.

With your group, ask each person in turn to comment on what they have noticed. They can't repeat but can add to another's observation. *What more can we find?* This brings out excitement and interest as new observations emerge. Both similarities and differences in perceptions and interpretations can generate discussion and further insight.

Slow looking can also encourage empathy. Ask your visitors to change their vantage point. *How might this indigenous people's mask feel to you if you wore it dancing in a ceremony? How might it feel to you if you were watching the ceremony?*

Jim Howard and Jack James, "Mask" A3404, Kwakwaka'wakw, photographed by Jessica Bushey. Courtesy of UBC Museum of Anthropology.

Touring an historical reconstruction, you could ask, *What would you be doing in the evening in this room/ cabin/shack/prison 200 years ago? What do you think an evening activity for kids might be in a migrant camp? An internment camp?*

Engage in artful thinking routines and activities
Artful thinking, as defined by Project Zero at the Harvard School of Education, is the "Focus on experiencing and appreciating art as a way to help students develop ways of thinking that support thoughtful learning." Many schools and museums around the country collaborate through on-site and virtual visits "to help teachers create connections between works of art and the curriculum and to help teachers use art as a force for developing students' thinking dispositions." Artful thinking strategies

are used in a wide variety of cultural, historical, and scientific institutions beyond art museums.

Our *Tours for Children and Teens* will describe several thinking routines drawn from the work of Project Zero educators and researchers. More information about Project Zero's work can be found at www.pz.gse.harvard.edu.

One commonly used artful-thinking routine is titled **See, Think, Wonder.** We ask three questions one after another:

What do you see?
What do you think about what you see?
What do you wonder about?

Project Zero explains: "This routine helps students make careful observations and develop their own ideas and interpretations based on what they see. By separating the two questions, What do you see? and What do you think about what you see? the routine helps students distinguish between observations and interpretations. By encouraging students to wonder and ask questions, the routine builds on curiosity and helps students reach for new connections."

Use hands-on objects and materials
Why provide additional material on a tour when our visitors can look at "the real thing" right in front of them? Hands-on means "touchable," when often museum collections and displays are strictly "do not touch." Being able to hold an object or view a photograph/video clip close up can heighten understanding and engagement in different ways.

Hands-on objects are typically reproductions or modern examples of what is on display or some detail of what is being viewed. Other common hands-on materials are photos and maps that may provide context or short videos and recordings to enhance an experience of the "silent" object.

Use hands-on materials in a tour to support your overall tour objectives and to engage your visitors in a thoughtful, selective way. Here are some reasons to include a hands-on activity.

You want to **encourage visitors to use other senses**— smell, hearing, touch—to connect with the displayed object.

- In a Silk Road exhibit, you pass around a piece of silk cloth.

- An outgrown snakeskin lets visitors touch and appreciate reptile growth processes.
- You play a brief recording of an ancient musical instrument.

You want to **promote close looking.**

- A close-up photo of a piece of actual lace shows what the artist's brushwork was depicting in a portrait.
- Ask your visitors to select three different red crayons/pencils/fabric swatches that match the reds in the abstract painting.
- Use cardboard "viewing tubes" for close inspection.

You want to provide a sense of the **object's original context**.

- Play a short video clip of Lindbergh landing in Paris while viewing his historic airplane.
- Pass around a photo of a religious object as it would be displayed or used originally.

You want to **explore the technology and production techniques** of an object.

- A short video of a calligrapher at work shows the artistry.
- Unfold a handscroll to demonstrate how it would be viewed.

Get visitors moving
Promote close looking by using movement and physical activity. Engaging young visitors in this way can help with the fidgets as well.

While looking at a statue or painting, ask your group to imitate the pose or poses of one or more of the figures.

- *Can you stand on one foot and raise your arms like the ballerina?*
- *Dig those potatoes! How would it feel to do that for hours and hours?*

Have the children sit on the floor in front of a large map of the area. *Who knows where the oldest house is on the map? Go stand there. How about our museum? Go stand there.*

Use stories
Telling stories and getting visitors to share the stories they see in the objects and artifacts we show them is an effective way to connect them to art, as well as to other cultural institutions such as historic houses and collections. In addition to the storytelling information in *The Docent Handbook 2,* we want to encourage visitors to find the stories in what they are viewing.

Here are some ideas:

- Talk about character, setting, and plot as the parts of a story, then ask students to find each one in the work at hand.
- Ask students what they think is happening in a work of art, then divide them into two groups to discuss what they think happened just before that moment and what will happen after. Have the two groups come together and discuss whether their versions of before and after mesh and if not, what each group saw that gave them a different interpretation. Or try with three groups—before, during, and after—rather than having a discussion of "during" with the whole group.
- Divide students into three groups, each with a supply of pencils and small blank cards. Assign a part of speech to each group—nouns, verbs, adjectives/adverbs. Give students 2-4 minutes to write as many words in their category that they see in the object at hand, one word per card. At the end of the time, ask students to work together to write a story using the cards they have written. Ask them to add whatever conjunctions, prepositions, and articles they need. Ask for feedback on the experience at the end.
- Ask students to "step inside" a painting and describe what they see, smell, hear and feel. Ask them to write or tell a story about their experience in the painting.
- Ask students to pick an object with one or more characters and make up a story about what those characters do at night when the museum is empty. For a gallery with many characters, ask the students to imagine what they say to each other when no one is around to hear them.

Stories help people remember and relate information. In addition to stories around the subject of an artwork or artifact, we can also tell stories about the object itself—how it was made, who made it, how it was used at the time it was made, how it got to the museum, and even what has happened to it in the museum if that is worthwhile. Storytelling fulfills a human impulse to communicate feelings and experiences. It is a way to make effective connections with our audience, including objects from an unfamiliar culture.

Make real-world connections to bring the museum experience into the lives of visitors.
A goal for every tour is to encourage personal connections to what is being viewed. Asking young visitors what they see in an abstract painting provides a way for them to connect to their own unique

perspective and experience and an opportunity for them to "own" the painting. Objects from long-ago times and different cultures can become relevant to kids today with some purposeful prompts. Viewing a formal European portrait, you can ask, *When do you put on your best clothes? What do they look like?* Looking at a display of a Native American ceremony you discuss how the regalia worn by the figures is made special. Then ask *What do you add to your clothing to make it special?*

Plan your tour with thought and care
Tours for children and teens require thoughtful preparation. Choosing a theme or guiding question with supporting objects, planning prompts and an activity, and collaboration with the teacher, if it is a school group, are essential. The topic of planning is so important that we cover it extensively in Chapter Two, "Getting Started."

Be flexible: blessed are the flexible for they shall not get bent out of shape
Things happen that can upend our best-laid tour plans. Common disrupters include:

- Students are interested in something other than what you had planned. Be prepared to make a short stop for an object that has attracted the group, tying it to your tour objectives. Then, if necessary, be clear in your reason for proceeding to the next planned stop.
- Students are so interested in one object that all your time in that gallery is used on that object. Congratulations, it must have been a rich exploration and discussion!
- A gallery you planned to use is unexpectedly closed to visitors.
- The docent ahead of you is still in the next gallery you are scheduled to use beyond the agreed-upon time.
- A student or chaperone suddenly becomes ill. Make sure you know your institution's policies for emergencies.
- Traffic or weather brings your group to the museum late. To the extent your own schedule allows, remember the often-daunting logistics teachers and adults face in getting to the museum and try to adjust the tour timing. If this interferes with another scheduled museum tour or event, let the teacher know the time limitations.
- Fewer students or chaperones arrive than planned. If more than one docent has been assigned, decide among yourselves if you each want smaller groups or if someone wants to bow out.

Each of these "disrupters" requires flexibility, quick thinking and calm.

Enjoy yourself!

We are docents because we love to share our enthusiasm for museums and the many kinds of cultural institutions suggested by that word. The most profoundly meaningful memories we take from our work, especially with children and teens, include the laughter, conversations, insights and discoveries made by young visitors. A key ingredient in any successful tour is the docent's joyful connection to the audience. Our goal is to show our visitors how much we enjoy and appreciate them and our time spent together in the museum.

YOUR PERSONAL NOTES

_____

_____

_____

_____

_____

_____

_____

_____

_____

_____

_____

_____

2 Getting Started

The Docent Handbook 2 includes useful general information about preparing and conducting any tour. Here, we provide information specific to tours for children and teens.

Know your audience

Most teachers expect their museum tour will connect to and reinforce their classroom studies. It is helpful to contact teachers in advance to ask about their goals for the tour and whether the students will have any assignments associated with the visit. *I would greatly appreciate your help to make sure this tour is as useful as possible to your students. How can I personalize this visit for you and make it relevant?*

Ask about proficiency in English and any physical or learning needs of the group. For tours that will require more than one docent, ask the teacher to divide the class into an appropriate number of groups in advance, each with an adult chaperone. If school policy allows, ask students to wear a name tag so they can be greeted personally. Ask teachers if they will be with the students on the tour, and if not, the name of the teacher who will accompany the group.

Most schools have a website and often a social media presence. Check them out to learn something about the school before your group arrives. For example, is there a band or choral group you could refer to in discussing a work that includes musical instruments or singing? You can personalize your greeting by welcoming students using the school's name and/ or mascot: *Welcome, Ravens! We're glad you're here today.*

The person requesting a tour for a home-schooled group can offer some of the same information as the school-based teacher. Often children of varying ages are part of the group, are used to working together, and enjoy off-site experiences. The tour leader may have suggestions specific to the group.

Family groups are typically informal, often part of a walk-in program, with no opportunity for the docent to have advance prior contact. The children may be of varying ages and family members may stretch across two or three generations. At the beginning of the tour, find out what each member hopes to see and do on the visit, if it is their first time in the museum, and other "getting to know you" information. All this can help guide the approach you use and the choices you make.

Plan your tour

In planning your tour, start with an essential question or theme. A theme or question provides a central idea to help explore and connect objects, to make comparisons, to shape transitions, and to summarize main points. A question that frames the tour as an issue to explore is helpful. Some examples might include:

- *How is "home" portrayed in images across the world?*
- *How do portraits create the idea of identity?*
- *What was the role of Colonial taverns at the beginning of the Revolutionary War?*
- *How do artists use the elements of art (line, form, shape, color, texture) to create images?*
- *How are animals used as symbols in different cultures?*
- *What should be the role of science in understanding our world?*
- *How can historical objects illuminate universal human rights?*

The questions you ask during the tour should be designed to help you and the students discover and explore answers to the key question. In the same way, a theme provides a central idea to be explored and elaborated on in the tour.

What are your main take-away ideas? The "rule of three"—a time-honored approach to speaking ("stop, look, and listen")—or having three main Ideas can be helpful here. Deciding on just a few basic points or ideas and reinforcing these with different stops and examples during the tour keeps you organized and makes it more likely your visitors will remember their experience.

> American history students visit a house museum that was formerly a tavern, or public house. Taverns in Colonial America often were multi-functional spaces—centers of food, drink, entertainment, socializing, debate, news from other colonies, mail distribution, boarding for travelers, meeting places for courts and assemblies, military recruitment, and small businesses. But what main ideas do you want students to take away if your theme involves the role taverns played in the beginning of the Revolutionary War? Your decision to focus on a limited number of key ideas will influence what students learn and remember.

Which objects/stops do you plan to include in your tour and are you clear about how they relate to each other and support your main ideas? For teens, where are you building in opportunities for their collaboration and choice? Think through the transitions from object to object and stop to stop. How are they connected? How will you tie the tour together at the end?

Decide on some possible questions and prompts to develop discussion and conversation in the group. Have more in mind than you will use. When a question falls flat, you will have another to try. Even the question that's most successful with one group may not work with another.

Plan your activities ahead of time, including hands-on materials, writing and sketching. As discussed in "Basics," activities support the overall objectives of the tour and increase your visitors' engagement. Be clear about the reasons for your choices. Too many activities may distract from your purpose. The "doing" should not become an end in itself; instead, let the activities support and enhance your main ideas.

Collaborate with other docents to develop your tour. Docents are often each other's best resource. What have other docents found helpful in tours with similar themes or objectives? Where will your group be in the museum? If other docents are sharing the tour with you, collaborate on the path each docent will take to

ensure time and space with key objects. Within your docent team, determine which hands-on materials to use on the tour and how they will be shared. If your museum allows, pre-position shared materials in front of relevant objects with a sign, "Materials for tours. Please do not disturb. Thank you!" Agree which docent will be responsible for picking up materials and signs.

Be sure to preview your tour path ahead of time to confirm that all the objects you plan to use are on view and the specific galleries are open.

Introduce yourself and your plan to your group

Tell something about yourself and the museum. Let your visitors know what they will be seeing on the tour and explain that you look forward to hearing their ideas. Introduce the tour theme or unifying idea/question. Connect it to any information you have from the teacher about what they are studying or hope to achieve. When your group arrives, check with the teacher/leader concerning the actual time available for the tour and establish where all participants should meet at the end. Point out the location (if any) where coats, lunches and backpacks can be left and where to find restrooms.

Clarify expectations with teachers, chaperones, and visitors

Meet any adult chaperones and request their specific assistance and support for the tour. You will want their help in keeping the group together. You may ask them to assist in handing out and collecting materials used on the tour and in accompanying younger children to restrooms. A floor plan of the museum with restrooms clearly marked is helpful to have with you.

Rules or expectations are important and can be incorporated in your welcome using positive language. For example, *Use your eyes to touch the things you see around you and not your hands.*

Determine whether children will have phones, and if so, the expectations (yours and the teacher's) for their use. Many school groups will not allow phones to be used; others may assign photo-taking to support classwork. When phones are permitted, a useful strategy is to allow a minute or two for photography at the end of tour stops.

Teens may be more likely to have and expect to use their phones for photos on the tour. Check with the accompanying teachers on their policy for the visit. Think through your approach to managing phone use ahead of time and communicate your expectation to the group at the beginning. Finding a fun and light-hearted way to incorporate phone use is a management strategy. You might suggest a group picture at a particular stop. Or ask that each person take a minute to send one text to someone with their personal take on a favorite object or to choose one object and take a selfie with it.

Ending your tour

Ask visitors to reflect on their experience with open-ended questions such as:

- *What was your favorite object/artwork/stop? Which was most surprising or memorable?*
- *What piece spoke most powerfully to you, considering our theme?*
- *Which one showed you something new?*
- *If you were telling someone about this tour, what object would you mention?*
- *If we had postcards or digital images of all the objects we've seen on this tour, which one would you want?*

If possible, leave the children and teens with something as a remembrance of the visit, whether a selfie, a photo, a sketch, or activity done in the museum, or a postcard, sticker, or brochure with contact information for the museum. Invite them to return to see more of the museum, to bring a friend or family member, or participate in an event or experience, both online and in-person.

YOUR PERSONAL NOTES

3 Tours with Younger Visitors

In this chapter we discuss and illustrate successful touring with our younger audiences. We use knowledge of age-specific developmental needs and accomplishments to craft information about touring strategies and approaches for Pre-K and K, first- and second- grade, and third- and fourth-grade groups. Many touring strategies discussed are relevant regardless of age or whether used in-person or for a virtual tour and are mentioned repeatedly. We explain these strategies with examples that illustrate what they "look like" and "sound like" depending on the ages of the participants. We supply practical and concrete information based on a solid understanding of the age or type of group throughout.

Youngest Visitors: Pre-K to K

Children in Pre-K and kindergarten are physically active learners, very much in the concrete stage of development. Play is the work of young children, and it is through play, either alone or with others, that children learn. Curiosity about the world in which they live leads to questioning everything and wanting to know the "hows" and "whys" of what they meet. These children are beginning to think symbolically and learning to use words and pictures to stand for objects. There are wide ranges in abilities as well as social and emotional maturity in this age range. Young children tend to be egocentric but are beginning to develop empathy on a simple level. Worrying about a classmate who is hurt or seeing a painting of a sad-looking child can elicit an emotional response. Most children of this age strive for the approval of the adults in their lives.

Young children typically have limited attention spans.

Therefore, a tour should not last longer than 45 minutes and should include only three stops.

A short, active tour helps children focus, get involved, and enjoy. It is difficult for the young child to maintain interest and excitement if a tour is too long. Children like to know what to expect, so it's useful to present them with a "picture schedule" at the start of the tour. Pictures of three objects help them see a beginning, middle and end and prepare them for what they will be seeing as they move around the museum. Choosing objects that are near eye level and large enough to be seen clearly helps keep their interest. Pick pieces that have enough space in front of them so children can sit comfortably to view the object.

Young children are active learners for whom play can be the gateway to learning. They learn best when something piques their interest and stimulates their imagination.

Therefore, more doing, less talking allows the young child to become more involved with the piece of art or other objects.

We touch materials that mimic those in the artifact - a furry cloth like the antique stuffed animal, or we put ourselves into a picture by taking a magical journey inside the painting. Once in it, we smell the aromas, make the sounds of the animals we see, get our feet wet in a stream, and get a close-up view of what the artist was trying to tell us. The goal is to keep the children actively engaged and involved with what they are seeing.

Help the children explore an object by giving them a moment to sit quietly and look at it, take a deep breath, and let it out as they focus on the work. As they look at the painting of a city, ask questions like, *Where do you think we are? How is this city street different from the one right outside the museum? What buildings did the artist put in this picture? Why do you think he put them in his painting? What buildings or places do we need where we live?* After talking about buildings and spaces that are important to our city, have them sit around a road map and design their very own block city. More doing!

Abstract art comes alive for young children when they are encouraged to use their imaginations and their bodies. Hands-on materials, movement and variety are key. They can form a tableau by waving colored scarves to create their own piece of art. For a fun activity, give the children colored pencils and paper and have them draw to music. They will love holding their creations up next to the museum object.

Young children learn best when something makes sense to them and in some way reflects their own experiences. We know that children at this age see the world as circling around them.

Therefore, we choose objects to which they can more easily relate.

Looking at a painting of young boy and his dog, we ask questions such as: *Who has a pet? How do you think this boy is feeling? What do you see that makes you think that? Who has ever felt the way this boy is feeling?* Young children will care about the boy and dog if they are helped to recall things that made them happy, sad, excited, curious or angry.

To further help them relate to the painting, have children pose like the boy and talk about how this makes them feel. Take the opportunity to talk about feelings and how our faces help show people what we are feeling inside. Use emotion picture cards (faces showing different emotions) so children can pretend to change the way this boy is feeling. As each card is held up, children change their own expression and tell how that makes them feel. Depending on the attention span of the group, expand this activity to include not just how you feel, but why you feel that way based on the painting.

These same activities may be adapted for museums that focus on history, culture, animals, and nature. When looking at a vignette of a colonial home, ask questions such as: *How is this room like a room where you live? Who do you think might live here? What do you think they might do for fun?* Or in an historic building point out the telephone hanging on the wall. Ask *How do phones in your home look? How do you think this old telephone worked?*

Young children are more engaged in learning when they are introduced to a variety of activities. The usual group time in a preschool is very brief and involves quiet and active experiences so short attention spans are not taxed.

Therefore, since we want this to be an enjoyable and informative adventure, books, songs and movement are integral parts of the tour. Using different media keeps up the tempo of the tour and gives the children many different experiences, all centered on a single theme.

One museum uses a "Dazzling Colors" theme with three- to five-year-old visitors. Guides begin with story time, reading aloud Pamela Duncan's *Warthogs Paint* about mixing primary colors (red, yellow, blue) to create surprising oranges, purples and greens. Children use color paddles (translucent primary-colored pieces of plastic) to mix and match and name their own color combinations. Then they go off to visit a Gene Davis painting dazzling with vertical pastel stripes. Lots of conversation follows about color and lines, and the words *vertical, repeat, stripe, pastel.*

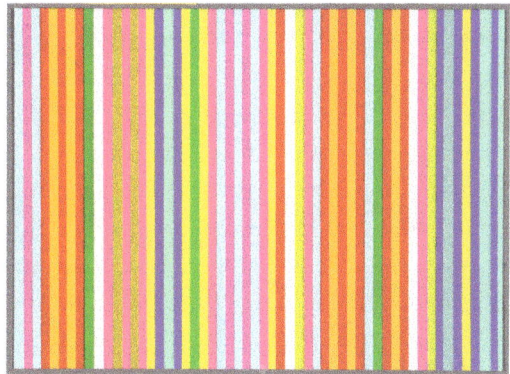

Gene Davis, "Powwow," 1969, screenprint on paper, Smithsonian American Art Museum, Bequest of Florence Coulson Davis

Enter the painting through the door of a single color. Can you squeeze through? Show me. Does your color have a name? Does the artist repeat the color anywhere else in the painting? How would you describe the color next door? Which of these colors have you made with your color paddles? What would you do with your stripe if you could grab hold of it? How would you change the order of the stripes?

After looking closely and talking about the abstract painting, these young visitors head to the studio for an art project. Paper, water, Cray-Pas (oil pastels to mix and blend colors), brushes and pens help children create their own "dazzling color" paintings to take home.

Choose books that are short, full of bright pictures, and lack a strict story line so that skipping pages does not detract from the reading. Books can be read at the start of the tour to help focus on the theme or later in the tour when they will refer more directly to an object or part of an exhibit.

Don't be afraid to break into song as the children stand in front of an object. Sing a song about kings and queens following a silly jester at a dance to discuss tempo and movement or sing a simple tune about looking for shapes on an Elements of Art tour.

Garden visits can be exciting for young ones. Ask the children to pretend that they are a flower. Walk them through the flower parts and associated motions, using language such as, *Plant your feet like roots, stretch up tall like a stem, use your palms like leaves to search for sunlight.* Ask students how being a flower feels or how the different parts of a plant work together to stay healthy. You can also expand this activity to talk about how the environment affects the way a plant grows. For example, flowers and trees will lean toward sunlight while in the shade. You can ask participants to bend and stretch like a tree reaching for sunlight, to twist like a vine climbing up a trellis, wave like grass in the wind, or bloom like a flower. As facilitator, you can "be the sun" and ask the students to bend in the direction of the sun.

Tudor Place Historic House and Garden, Washington, DC. With permission.

A song about textures can help introduce that concept. *Put your hand on your hair, on your hair; Put your hand on your face, on your face; Put your hand on the floor and put it there once more; Put your hand on your hair, on your hair.* This is followed by the questions: *When you touched these things, did they feel the same? Which felt smooth? Which felt rough? The way things feel when you touch them is called texture.* A texture bag filled with materials that feel like how the objects in the paintings might feel is a good complement to the song. Children are encouraged to put their hand in the bag, pull something out, describe its texture and then find something in the picture or on the sculpture that might feel like it. This is how children get to feel the art without touching it!

As much as possible, the art experience should be active and hands-on. Use movement to stimulate ideas and curiosity.

In zoos or natural history museums, you can ask kids to wiggle like snakes being coaxed out of a basket or stomp around like very large hippos. Move like monkeys swinging from branch to branch or the elephant searching for tasty grass with her trunk. No time to lose interest!

Museums, with their art-covered walls, object-filled spaces, and large, sometimes cavernous rooms can be unsettling to young children. With so much to see, it is difficult for this age to concentrate on a particular object and give it and the docent their full attention.

Therefore, when moving from space to space, we engage the children in an activity related to the theme of the tour.

Use the tour theme as a starting point; don't just walk from one object to the next. If the theme is Animals in Art, move from gallery to gallery as creeping lions, soaring birds or long-necked giraffes.

On a tour devoted to the Elements of Art, move as various kinds of lines. Holding up a picture of a line and challenging the children to move in that way makes the journey more interesting even as they are learning about one of the elements of art. Moving as a dotted line is so much more fun than simply walking to the next painting.

After seeing an art object showing a parade, become the parade. The children are so busy marching that they are not overwhelmed by the spaces.

Grades 1 and 2

Children at this age are more independent and seem more open to new experiences while still seeking the approval of adults in their lives. Even though they are more proficient in using language to communicate, they still tend to think about things in concrete terms. These children have also become more skilled at pretend play. They may have difficulty with logic and accepting the point of view of others. As a group they are more socially comfortable, but they represent a wide range in abilities as well as social and emotional maturity. Many of the touring suggestions for working with three- to five-year-old children also apply to this age group. The main difference is that the docent can add more detail to the presentation and not include an involved activity at every stop.

Children of this age still typically have a limited attention span.

Therefore, tours should not exceed one hour and should include activities as well as adequate time to concentrate on an object.

Since children are more comfortable in a new situation when they know what to expect, present them with either a visual or oral schedule at the start of the tour. Also, choose objects that are close to the eye level of the children and large enough to be seen clearly. Pick pieces with enough space around them so children can sit comfortably to view the object. Have a theme connecting all the objects so that the tour makes sense to the children. For example, create an Animals in Art tour, where each stop involves either real or imaginary animals.

First and second graders are more independent and pay more attention to friendships and teamwork. They have less focus on self and more concern for others.

Therefore, there should be some interactive experiences within the framework of the tour.

After looking at a work of art that contains human and animal figures, what better way to get children to jump into the painting than by creating their own tableau? Give each child or pair of children a picture of one of the characters. After they have located their character, they can pose as that character and even talk about what they are doing and what is going on around them. This activity can be done in an interview format with either the docent or a child holding a "microphone" and

questioning the character. The cardboard tube from a roll of paper towels makes a perfect "microphone." Since the children are more social at this stage, they may also be encouraged to have a conversation, in character.

Another way to engage children and have them work together is to create a group story. After looking at an object, the docent might start with something like, *I had a dream last night about……* after which each child, in turn, may add something to the story related to what they think the object is telling them. Or have each child work with a partner to find a particular object or color or shape in an artwork. This provides children independence as well as an opportunity to collaborate with another child.

Finally, the popular game *I Spy* makes for a lively and focused activity in front of a work of art. Here is an example of *I Spy*. The docent points to the picture and describes something that they see: *I spy with my little eye something that is red and has a stem* (an apple). The children then find the object and discuss why they think it was put in the work. The first child to find the object could have the next turn in the game.

Children of this age typically show rapid development of mental skills.

Therefore, it is important that we give them the opportunity to exercise their minds by challenging them to figure out what the artist wanted us to see or how the artist made an object.

Look at either an abstract or representational painting and after studying the work, present the children with an Artist's Toolbox (shoebox filled with shapes, types of lines, colors, and textures). Zero in on two or three of the elements that artists use to create art. Have children explore the colors that were used. Were they primary colors or were they made by combining two colors? Using color paddles allows them to create their own colors by placing one paddle on top of the other and looking through them. What fun it is to discover that when you put a yellow paddle on top of a red one, you see orange!

Ask what lines they can find in the painting and have them use pipe cleaners to duplicate those lines. Have the children look for textures in a piece of art by pulling different materials out of the box. Ask them to use their imaginations to figure out what things represented in the painting (or sculpture) might have this texture if they were real. Using the vocabulary for textures can open a lively discussion about the descriptions of how something feels.

Pass around a piece of jade and a piece of bamboo and show how ancient artists had to rub away the stone with coarse paste to create the ornament. *How long would it take, do you think?*

Children of this age understand more about their place in the world. They also learn new ways to describe experiences and talk about thoughts and feelings.

Therefore, it is important to have many open-ended questions that allow the children to express themselves and explain what they are seeing.

Introduce an art museum tour as one where visitors are encouraged to look at a piece of art and describe what it means to them. There are no wrong answers when you interpret a drawing, painting or sculpture.

Start by having children zoom in slowly with their eyes and then zoom back out as they look at an object. Ask open-ended questions:

- *What do you think is happening in this painting?*
- *What do you see that makes you think that?*
- *How does this piece of art make you feel?*
- If there are figures in the artwork, ask, *How do you think they are feeling? What do you see that makes you think that?* This activity helps children understand that looking at art is personal and based on their own experiences.

For tours in museums devoted to history, animals, transportation or cultures, there may be right and wrong answers. However, we can still give children a chance to exercise their observational skills and make their own judgments. Looking at a display of Ancient Egyptian items of daily living gives children the opportunity to examine an object visually and try to figure out what it is, how it was used, and what we use today for a similar purpose. If given time and encouragement to come up with their own ideas and answers, it is their reasoning, not their answers, that is the important outcome of this activity.

Children like to hear the science or history behind the exhibit, the real story, but learn even more when they are given permission to share what they think without judgment.

Children visit a natural history museum to see an insect zoo and butterfly pavilion. Docents are "insect ambassadors" whose objects are alive, interactive and constantly changing. Carts, windows and feeding stations encourage young visitors to observe closely, make comparisons, ask questions, and even to interact with some of the invertebrates, such as grasshoppers, praying mantises, spiders and butterflies. Some questions to guide children's observations include:

- *How would you describe this insect's body?*
- *How do you think this insect would feel if you could touch it?*
- *Why do you think this insect is called a walking stick?*
- *How do you think this insect protects itself?*

Children hear specific language related to insects and expand their vocabulary: cocoon, chrysalis, venom, exoskeleton, pollinator. In a setting that inspires such wonder, "ambassadors" lead children to question and explain what they're seeing and to make connections to their own lives. Big overarching questions such as, *How are insects helpful?* can lead to more specific discussions and questions answered through observation and modeling.

When children combine their observational skills with information and guiding questions from docents, they develop working hypotheses based on evidence. In a butterfly pavilion, an iPad can show the anatomy of a butterfly. Then, watching a monarch use its proboscis to suck up juice from a cantaloupe is a memorable and powerful way to address the question, *Do butterflies have mouths?* With hands-on experiences like these, first- and second-graders work to develop their reasoning skills and reach their own conclusions.

Grades 3 to 6

Older elementary children seem to grow and change by the week and seldom in predictable or consistent ways. They are alternately giggly and pensive, altruistic and self-centered, assertive and shy, in constant motion and seemingly exhausted. Being treated fairly is in the forefront of their minds. How many times have we heard "It's not fair" being applied to siblings, classmates and privileges? Their heroes tend to be family members, media or sports stars, rescuers, and kid heroes real and imagined, such as Malala Yousafzai and Harry Potter. Eight- to twelve-year-olds are learning to step into others' shoes and will respond positively to stories about people who demonstrate empathy. They are on the cusp of becoming abstract thinkers, but a wide range still exists in their ability to grasp metaphor and abstract concepts.

Third to sixth graders are eager to explore, discover and learn.

Therefore, museum tours should use a variety of methods to encourage engaged participation with children this age, such as close looking and open-ended questions.

Eight- to twelve-year-olds are particularly well-suited to looking closely, thinking about what they see and hear, and wondering about what's going on. They are increasingly observant, attentive, articulate, empathetic, and quite un-self-conscious within their peer groups. They enjoy partnering or forming small groups to accomplish a task and are learning to collaborate. They respond to questions that invite a wide variety of responses and active participation in discussions.

Animals in Art is a compelling and popular museum subject for children in this age group. We often prompt animated conversations when we examine two- and three-dimensional representations of real and imaginary animals, compare their features, and wonder about their attributes.

- *How dangerous do you think it might feel to get close to this ancient bronze sculpture of a tiger? Why do you think the sculptor tried to make this creature look scary?*
- *This tiger was made for the entrance to a tomb. What do you think the effect might have been on someone trying to get inside the tomb? Let's compare the bronze tiger with a painted ceramic guardian figure made up of parts from several different animals.*
- *As we look at other animals, such as a carved jade dragon or a bronze bird, think about what qualities an animal would need to make it a guardian figure. What questions would you ask to help you decide?*

Continue to explore and discuss several other museum creatures, noticing features and attributes, finding favorites, distinguishing between depictions of real and imaginary creatures, pondering what each was used for.

- *Which might have been guardians? Why? What other roles might these animals have played?*

As a follow-up, try a short art activity. Ask children to select some favorite features of real and imagined animals to create a guardian figure of their own. Where would they place their animal guardian?

Third to sixth graders are interested in why and how things were made, how long it took to make them, and if utilitarian, how they were used.

Therefore, demonstrating with hands-on materials, modeling and role-playing help children explore the process of creation. Understanding how things are made offers clues to meaning and use.

Children this age wonder how robots work, who invented toothpaste, why pyramids were built, who wrote the dictionary. They are interested in fossils, artifacts, inventions and science fiction. They are beginning to have a more specific sense of time than "long ago," "now," or "in the future." One way to provide touchstones for their growing understanding of timelines is to examine and discuss representative objects from previous eras. Exploring the "why and how" behind artworks and artifacts offers a peek into the creative process.

This is an age when children are interested in collecting objects and images, such as stuffed animals, trading cards, shells and posters. Some collectibles include homemade items, such as painted rocks. Most children in this age group have become skilled observers of similarities and differences.

Therefore, visiting museums to learn about collections that focus on art, history, natural history, science, technology, sport, and many other topics is intriguing to this age group. How, when, and by whom were the objects collected? How does the museum care for and display the objects?

Looking at a quilt from the 19th or early 20th century lets us talk about aspects of American history, geography, geometry, craft and elements of art such as color, line, shape, texture and composition. This makes quilts ideal objects for investigation about the creative process. As children look closely at examples of quilts, we guide their attention with questions, such as:

- *What kinds of patterns do you notice? Can you find examples of symmetry? Asymmetry?*
- *Many quilt patterns had names, like Flying Geese and Log Cabin. What names would you use for these quilts?*
- *The colored fabric often is cut from used clothing so nothing goes to waste. An earlier version of recycling! Where do you think these fabrics might have come from? What fabric scraps would you use to make a quilt of your own?*

American Doll Quilt, Pieced and tied fabric, Early 20th century. Private collection

What clues suggest how these quilts were made? It may surprise you to learn that quilts are like sandwiches... Describe and demonstrate the layers of a quilt to help explain their use as bedcovers, the "sandwich" of layers adding warmth to winter beds. The process of creation sometimes is a communal one, as when several people contribute to the "quilting bee."

- *What other forms of creative expression might include a community of makers?* (Chinese scrolls; pottery; bronze sculptures; printmaking; dance; music making...)

Museums inspire children to curate their own collections. An exhibition of artworks by a single artist helps young visitors notice changes in style, experimentation with different materials, and varieties of subject matter. Collecting images of works by a favorite artist might result. Rock collections in a natural history museum inspire youngsters to identify and classify specimens from different geologic ages and regions. As children notice the differences among igneous, metamorphic, and sedimentary rocks on display, they may want to reorganize their own collections. Various flying vehicles on display in an air and space museum or cars in an antique auto museum might motivate a youngster to build and collect models.

Ask questions that guide children to sort, categorize and evaluate. Encourage children to share their observations with a classmate in a turn-and-talk activity, which may lead to further discoveries. Divide children into small groups and give each group a bag of objects, like different-sized and shaped seashells. Ask each group to decide how they would organize the collection, then share their decisions with the whole tour group. Information about a donor or collectors can be woven into the discussion. Old or fragile objects that require museum conservation offer other avenues for exploration.

Often museums feature an exhibition organized around the donated objects of an individual collector or family. As children examine the exhibit, ask:

- *What seems to fascinate this collector?*
- *How are the objects similar or different?*
- *As you look more closely, what catches your attention?*
- *From what you see, does anything seem to be missing from this collection? What would you add? Does the exhibit give you any ideas for displaying your own collection? What are some ways you take care of your collection?*

Often specific exhibits are organized around themes or subject matter, displaying objects from many collectors, for example, sports museums or portrait galleries. You could guide the discussion to focus on the shared interests of a group of collectors and donors.

- *What would these collectors talk about if we could put them together in the same room?*
- *Why might it be hard for one collector to gather all these objects into one collection?*

As a follow-up and in collaboration with the visiting teacher, children might curate a museum display at home or at school.

> One class visited a portrait gallery and focused on Hispanic and Latinx leaders. With the help of classroom and Spanish teachers at school, children created a tribute to relatives who had passed away by mounting a museum wall of photographs and drawings to celebrate *Dia de los Muertos*, the Mexican Festival of the Dead. In a colorful celebration of love and respect for deceased family members, children crafted decorative frames, lively "wall chats," endearing titles, and a short gallery guide to the exhibit.

Many third to sixth graders enjoy stories such as traditional tales and historical fiction, contemporary stories and futuristic fiction. They can distinguish between the imaginary world and perceived reality and are developing a greater awareness of and appreciation for facts.

Therefore, storytelling provides an avenue to weave factual information into stories that are part of the object's cultural heritage.

Good stories contain layers of meaning that children can peel away at their pleasure. Developmental levels are just one factor among many that determine how deeply children can access meaning from art and literature. Younger children in this age group likely will connect their personal experiences to what they see and hear; older children may attach more metaphorical and abstract meanings to stories.

Take, for example, the global appeal of magic and folktales. Younger children probably won't connect with the "unjust oppression and triumphant reward" of the Cinderella character but will enjoy the rags-to-riches story. Harry Potter fans often focus on the action and adventure, the magical creatures and brave deeds. Mature readers also appreciate the complex nature of the relationships and the characters' struggles to reckon with their humanity. Some museum objects are enhanced by the stories that inspired them, and young visitors make deeper connections as they enjoy stories

The Chinese artist Xu Bing created an 80-foot-long hanging sculpture that extends from the museum atrium skylight to the basement reflecting pool, *Monkeys Grasp for the Moon*. Xu Bing's monkeys are created from interpretations of the word *monkey* in twenty-one different languages. His inspiration was a traditional Buddhist folktale about monkeys who look down from a tall tree to see the moon in a pool of water far below. They work together to link their arms and tails into a chain to replace the moon in the night sky. But when the littlest monkey touches the water, the shimmery illusion disappears.

Xu Bing, "Monkeys Grasp for the Moon," 2004, Xu Bing / Arthur M. Sackler Gallery, Smithsonian Institution, Washington, D.C.: Purchase – funds provided by the family of Madame Chiang Kai-shek (Chiang Soong Mayling 1898-2003), S2004.2.1-21

Eight- to twelve-year-olds uncover the layers of meaning in the monkey chain in several ways. But without the story, the sculpture is simply an intriguing collection of intricately carved black shapes that represent "monkey." With the story, we may ask questions to encourage conversations about cooperation, connections between words and images, global languages, illusion versus reality.

• *What do you think this folktale means?*
• *What lessons can we learn from this story?*
• *Why do you think Xu Bing used many languages to depict the monkeys?*
• *What connections to common themes or traditions do you recognize?*

alongside observations, facts and questions about the piece.

Third to sixth graders grow more thoughtful about issues of fairness and move from personal and local concerns to more broadly national and global issues.

Therefore, engaging children in early discussions about issues such as sustainability, food insecurity, habitat preservation and human rights helps build awareness and empathy.

Many children in this age group are social and environmental activists. They help their families recycle, make sandwiches for soup kitchens, and work on behalf of animal adoption. They are interested in endangered animals and clean rivers. Children may experience hunger, homelessness and violence and have a realistic view of problems in everyday life. They are becoming aware of issues that will affect the world they are about to inherit. Museums and zoos can help elementary-aged children ask big questions such as, *Where can we make a difference?* and *Well, why not?*

Edward Hicks, "Peaceable Kingdom," ca. 1830-1832, Metropolitan Museum of Art

Children who focus on the details in Edward Hicks's oil painting *Peaceable Kingdom* (1830-32) might wonder about the unlikely group of animals—a lion with an ox, a leopard with a lamb—resting in a forest with a child standing among them. Concluding with the question, *What do you think the Quaker preacher, Edward Hicks, hoped to express in this painting?* could lead to discussions about peaceful resolutions of differences and the role children can play in bringing about change.

In one western state, fourth graders complement their state studies by visiting, either in-person or virtually, an early 19th-century ranch that serves as a microcosm of regional history. The site includes an adobe house, gardens, barns, fields, and outbuildings such as a blacksmith shop. Students might visit the map room, library, schoolroom, kitchen and working barn. Docents introduce children to the intersecting and diverse lives of workers, tenants and lease farmers, and owners who arrived from around the world and from within our country: China, Japan, Europe, Mexico, native peoples and White settlers, many working to make productive lives for themselves and their families, some trying to protect sacred lands. Docents ask questions that develop awareness and empathy for complex relationships in the past while building connections to the present.

- *How might your understanding of an unfamiliar culture change if you learned songs or heard stories from someone on the ranch from a different part of the world?*
- *How does your understanding change about a culture other than your own when you learn some of the language and traditions of that culture?*

Tours with Children and Teens Handbook

YOUR PERSONAL NOTES

4 Tours with Teens

In this chapter we consider tours for our older school-aged visitors. We divide the teen years into younger and older, representing middle school and high school students in most jurisdictions. There are gains in maturity and cognitive abilities as the teen years progress, and we have reflected this in our strategies and suggestions. As in the previous chapter, we begin with statements of general age-relevant development, followed by implications for touring and tour interaction.

Young teens: Grades 7 and 8

Young adolescents are going through physical, mental, emotional and social changes. While they often may be curious and fun-loving, they also tend to be self-conscious, moody and restless. It is a time of uneven growth in all areas. You can expect a wide range of developmental levels within one group of students.

Childhood has just been left behind; maturity beckons. These young people are expanding their range of interests and growing their ability for abstract thinking. They also are egocentric, intensely interested in themselves and their peers. They are better able to talk through their feelings and ideas. They exercise increasing independence, and a museum trip is a welcome change from the routines of school. While heavily influenced by peer pressure and wanting to fit in, young teens also want to feel special and unique.

Young adolescents can feel awkward and unsure in new situations and may revert to less mature behaviors or silence in response. They want to be liked by authority figures even while testing them.

Therefore, we do not take personally eye-rolling, showing off, silliness or wandering attention; rather, we understand this as sometimes typical for the age group. We work to be friendly and interested in them personally, to keep a sense of fun and humor, while setting necessary limits and providing structure.

Oh no, I've been assigned a group of 7th-graders. Such a refrain might come from even the most experienced docent. Why is this? Sometimes this cluster of "negative" behaviors discourages and even upsets docents. Or a group may greet you with silence and signs of resistance. Remember this is typical and should be understood as a normal response to feeling awkward and unsure.

The first step to successfully engaging your group is to welcome them warmly, personalize your introductions, and let them know just what to expect during your time together.

- *What's your favorite thing about your school?*
- *What other field trips do you take?*
- *Our topic today is one of my favorites. May I tell you why?*

Let them know what they are going to encounter on the tour and what to expect in the way of discussion and activities. As the tour progresses, listen carefully to what they say and accept comments, even if they seem silly and/or off topic. Don't challenge or correct their logic. Ask them to explain how they came to that idea.

- *I'm interested that this reminds you of a video game. Tell us about the connection for you.*
- *You disagree that this face mask from the Lele people of the Democratic Republic of the Congo could have been impressive. What change would make it impressive, do you think? If you were a villager watching, how might your reaction be different? What do others think?*

As with any age group, tours with younger teens present opportunities for success as well as challenges. Design your tour to encourage a real sense of competence among the teens, for example, by pairing students or forming small working groups. Use humor when appropriate; point out surprising or amusing aspects of objects or comment on an artist's sense of whimsy, irony or comedy. Show your good nature without abandoning your authority.

This age group has increased capacity for initiative and responsibility.

Therefore, we design tours to provide roles and tasks for students, spreading them around the entire group. We give students opportunities to share in the process of the tour.

Organize your tour so that young teens become participants and collaborators. Depending on the group and guidance from teachers, the tour might be more or less structured. For example, at some point in the tour you might use the technique of guided discovery. Ask individual students or groups of two or three students to select an object from a room or an exhibit, explain their choice, and pose a question about the piece. The docent and students can weave a theme from the connecting threads among the choices. Students likely will feel real ownership of their tour.

Students from a world history class examined art objects from the Islamic world. One group focused on a 14th-century Egyptian glass mosque lamp painted with an inscription from the Qur'an. They had text information to guide them, along with a close-looking routine. They made sketches of the lamp and listed questions about its use in a mosque. When the class rejoined the docent, each group summed up its observations and discussed the imagery of the whole piece.

Mosque Lamp, Mamluk period ca. 1360, Freer Gallery of Art, Smithsonian Institution, Washington, D.C.: Purchase – Charles Lang Freer Endowment, F1957.19

- *Look around this gallery and choose an object that makes you want to know how it was made. Which one might have been hardest to make? Come back with your question.*
- *Look around and choose an object in the gallery that tells us something about you.*
- *Which object would you like to give to someone?*
- On an art museum tour, you can give each student one of three cards labeled "color," "shape" and "line." At different artworks, ask the students with the card "color" to share their observations with the group. Continue with "shape" and "line." Ask the whole group if there is anything they would add to the analysis of art elements.

A more structured tour also can offer opportunities for meaningful collaboration and engagement.

Visitors in this age group are learning to deal with complexity in many of their school studies. Young teens have broadened intellectual interests and curiosity, often leading them to question more extensively. They use their growing analytical skills and increased capacity to understand nuance.

Therefore, we ask challenging and thought-provoking questions with no right answer. We encourage them to explore different perspectives, relationships among parts, and changes over time.

Ask challenging questions that are specific to the object, not just *What do you notice?*

- *Where do you see the artist using patterns? What does that contribute to the composition?*
- *What do you think makes this portrait "presidential" (royal, impressive)?*
- *Why do you think a powerful person would want to be buried with this object?*
- *What do you think the Haida owner of this totem pole was telling his community? Can you tell us more about your thinking? How do we send messages about ourselves/family to our neighbors today?*

Ask for close looking and more extensive analysis of an object or consideration of an issue.

- *What do you see going on here? What suggests that to you? What else is happening? Is there anything you find puzzling in this scene?*
- *What does this reconstructed slave quarter hut suggest were the challenges to daily household living? What does that have to say about the lives of the enslaved? Of the enslavers?*

- *What message do you think the nature photographer is sending in this photo? Do you think the message would change if you photographed this scene today? How so?*
- *Who do you think made this object and what was that person(s) like? Why do you think it was made?*

Directly communicate your knowledge and appreciation of their abilities to think, observe and make connections, which reinforces competent, on-target behaviors.

- *I never noticed that before. Thank you for pointing that out.*
- *Interesting connection. Other ideas?*
- *Have you seen anything like... before? Where?*

Objects can be rich in hidden stories. A group examines this silver chocolate pot, finding more than the French rococo style. Discussing the origin of chocolate in South America, students think about the conquest of indigenous peoples by Europeans. They also discuss the story of enslaved people who raised sugarcane and changed sugar from a luxury to an affordable ingredient, laying the groundwork for its current saturation of the American diet and epidemic of obesity and diabetes.

Joseph-Théodore Van Cauwenbergh, Chocolate Pot, 1774, silver, amaranth wood. Museum purchase with funds provided by the S. & A.P. Fund, 1948, acc. no. 57.1802. Photo courtesy of The Walters Art Museum, Baltimore

Encourage thinking about multiple points of view. Viewing a photograph of an historic house museum's 19th-century African-American gardener, students are asked, *Whose history is saved? What do we learn about this man from the photo? What can't we learn? Historically, whose stories or perspectives were more likely to be saved and shared? Whose stories are we saving today?*

We know young teens are quite preoccupied with self and tend to respond to museum visits through their own feelings, ideas and life experience.

Therefore, we ask for their views, ideas and preferences. We look for ways to connect what they are viewing to their own lives and interests.

We validate their personal responses wholeheartedly.

- *I can see your point of view on this piece. You've based it on close looking*

Think about how a selected object can provide a pathway from one culture or time to their own. How can students see themselves and their reality in what they are viewing?

- A multimedia exhibit of American Indian art includes 19th century photographs of government-run boarding schools intended to assimilate Indigenous children. After close looking and discussion, a guide might ask, *What would you miss most if you were suddenly separated from your family and community? How does the exhibit add to your understanding of the American experience?*
- Touring a group in the 19th-century English portrait gallery, the docent asks the students to choose a painting and create its hashtag. Or the docent asks students to describe how they would want to be portrayed in a portrait—what clothes they would wear, where they would be, what objects would be in the portrait with them—or how selfies compare to these painted portraits.
- *What would you find hardest if you were in the Space Station for many months at a time?*
- While visiting the kitchen of a 19th-century historic house, ask: *What foods could you not live without?* Or at a farm museum: *What chores do you have at home? What do you think it would be like to be thirteen and growing up on this farm?*

Finally, your genuine interest in these young teens' observations and responses, whether singly or in small groups, will encourage their view that this museum visit is a fun and special event and deserves attention and participation. If disruptions or disengagements occur, acknowledge the behaviors with reminders about demonstrating their respect for each other, for you, and for the museum.

• *OK, everyone. Let's regroup for a minute. I know you have plenty of ideas and thoughts to share and that you are respectful of each other. Let's try exploring this gallery/object/… again, this time listening to each other and giving it what I know is your best.*

Older teens: Grades 9 to 12

High school students bring knowledge, curiosity and experience to their museum visit along with an awareness of social, environmental and ethical issues that affect their communities, nation and the world. They comprise the "app generation" and are well-acquainted with social media, online research, chat rooms, messaging and virtual learning. Many high schoolers are experienced collaborators, flexible thinkers, proficient in more than one language, and committed to high ideals.

These young adults often wish to make their museum experience meaningful on their terms, alone or with a small group of friends. Protocols, routines, whole group experiences, or lectures may not appeal to them. Working closely with their teacher to connect the tour to their interests and assignments will be important. Encourage autonomy and flexibility within the tour structure to help make the experience engaging and relevant.

These teens look to their group for their sense of personal safety; peer influence and acceptance are important.

Therefore, we understand initial reluctance for anyone to "stand out" and risk looking foolish to the group, and that aloof behavior may be typical. We work to create individual comfort as well as a functioning group.

To break the ice, introduce yourself briefly with a bit of personal information, such as why you are a docent/ guide at this museum. Ask students to introduce themselves (a way to ensure that each teen speaks at least once) and to describe their goals in visiting the museum. *I'm interested in what each of you enjoys in the class you're taking that brings you to the museum today.* Encourage conversations about other museum visits. Be friendly and be yourself. Don't try to be a peer. Aim to balance group cohesion with individual expressions and contributions. Initial reluctance to speak in front

A class of Chinese Studies students examined a freestanding sculpture of the Cosmic Buddha, which is inscribed with stories from the life of the Buddha. Mapped images of the figure's varied sections were handed out to pairs of students who interpreted their scene based on close looking and a previous introduction to the Buddha's life. When the class regrouped around the sculpture, teams compared notes, decided on the sequence of events from birth to death, and narrated the story while pointing to the artwork. The docent provided direction, guidance and encouragement throughout, but the students essentially became their own docents.

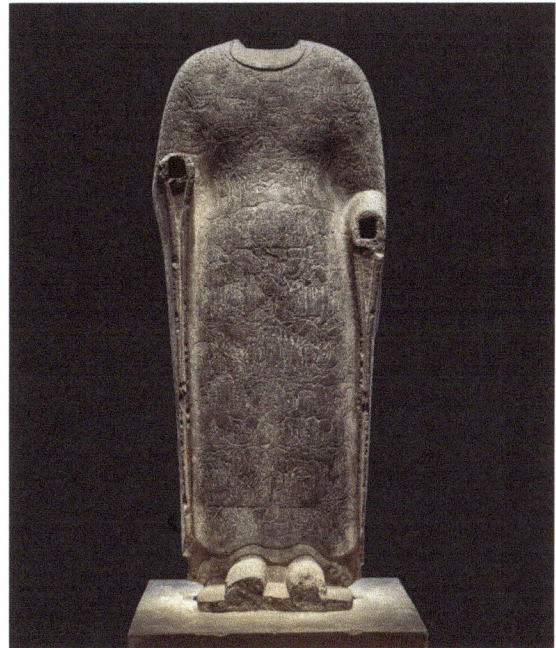

Buddha draped in robes portraying the Realms of Existence, Northern Qi Dynasty, 550-577, Freer Gallery of Art, Smithsonian Institution, Washington, D.C.: Purchase – Charles Lang Freer Endowment, F1923.15

Panel from the Sculpture above, showing one of the realms. Freer Gallery of Art, Smithsonian Institution, Washington, D.C.: Purchase – Charles Lang Freer Endowment, F1923.15 (Detail)

of peers in a new setting may be alleviated by your strategies to put teens at ease.

Don't take personally behaviors that may feel off-putting. Don't let body language get you down. Since teens may be reticent about starting to talk, recognize that silence may signify safety. Indicating your interest in each group member's idea/response helps reduce discomfort. Giving students lead time can help. *Here is a question to think about as we move to the next object.*

High school teens want to know they are liked and respected by an adult authority. They want to be collaborators and engage with docents/guides, as with adults in general, in ways that respect their maturity, knowledge and opinions.

Therefore, we design our tour to provide elements of choice and opportunities for collaboration to acknowledge these older teens' autonomy.

When time and teacher interest allow, many museums' on-line collection resources can be used before the tour. In keeping with the tour theme, you can provide a list of objects with their images in advance. Ask each student to choose an object for quick research and to present to others in the group during the tour.

Strive to be a facilitator on the tour, giving up the "authority/expert" role. Encourage the students to be co-contributors. Build in opportunities at different points in the tour for them to select objects of interest, individually or as a group. Slow down; allow silence and extended looking. Let students examine objects without explaining. Use open-ended questions and validate all responses. Ask for other group members' responses or opinions about what a classmate notices, encouraging dialogue. Promote slow looking through questions that require observation, thinking, reflection.

- *Look around. What object makes you curious about how it was made?*
- *Which object do you consider beautiful?*
- *Which object would you choose to give to someone to solve a problem or concern they are having?*
- *Which object makes you uncomfortable?*

These teens have rapidly developing logical and analytic skills and are eager to use them. They can consider many points of view.

Therefore, we use questions to probe for reasoning behind responses. We can ask this age group to make more detailed and complex observations and

A "Silk Road" tour for a summer teen group began with the idea of how transfers of goods and ideas influence creative output. *In what ways is cultural exchange expressed through art?* The students examined objects from China, India, ancient Gandhara (Pakistan) and Central Asia to search for evidence of the intermingling and transmission of design, themes, technology and materials. A Buddhist statue from Gandhara shows the influence of classic Greek sculptural style, a result of Greek artists who followed Alexander the Great after his conquest of the region. Students are asked: *What are some things we enjoy today and are popular in this country that have been transferred to us by other cultures? How did it happen?*

Gandharan, "Buddha Preaching," 3rd century CE, schist. Gift of John and Berthe Ford, 1912, acc. no. 25.266. Photo courtesy of The Walters Art Museum, Baltimore

interpretations, requiring more nuanced thinking about possibilities. We encourage comparing or debating ideas and opinions.

As you plan your tour, think about the broader ideas that exist behind the objects, expanding the focus beyond specific facts and descriptions. Be genuinely curious about what they think and encourage elaboration.

- *What makes something historically important? Of value to a culture? What makes something a work of art?*
- *Does art need to be beautiful? Why or why not?*
- *Should the owner/maker of an object or the viewer determine "meaning" in a work?*

Tours with Children and Teens Handbook

- *This object was created for a temple/wealthy home/ burial site. If you saw it there, what might your feeling/reaction have been? How is it different in a museum setting?*
- *Does 'sacred' always mean the same thing? What makes an object sacred?*
- *What can this painting tell us about social conditions at that time?*
- *Of the works you looked at, which do you most relate to? Why?*
- *How does portrayal of the sitter change over time in portraits?*
- *What questions do you still have?*
- *What new perspectives did you hear from classmates today? Can you relate?*

Older adolescents have a growing awareness and curiosity about contemporary social and cultural issues as well as traditions.

Therefore, we tap into their existing knowledge and understanding of these issues in connection with their lived experiences and build on their empathy, curiosity, and perspective-taking.

These teens often have thought deeply about global challenges such as racial justice, gender identity, environmental protection, politics and patriotism.

- *Which object/painting raises a global concern for you? Does it suggest a human rights or environmental concern?*
- *Which work felt most relevant to our world today? Why?*
- *What do you think characterizes this object as part of Latinx/Black/Islamic/ Buddhist/European... culture? How do you think the artist/creator of this object intended the viewer to respond, and why?*
- *What was your initial reaction to this object? How do you think you might react if you were from another culture?*
- *You have noticed this figure looks both like a man and woman. Does it make a difference which gender is portrayed? Why might gender identity here be ambiguous?*

Visits to historical museums and sites can bring up controversial contemporary topics in American history. Owners of historical houses may have enslaved people, and the realities of their acquiring and selling people, including separation of families, as well as how the enslaved supported the life and livelihood of the enslavers can be explored in the context of social justice realities today.

Know your audience and consult with teachers before addressing sensitive topics, but these older teens may find exchanges deeply meaningful in exhibits designed to present information in clear, relevant ways. For example, American history museum tours might include conversations about the removal of Civil War statues, about the social and economic impact of consumer goods, about immigration history, or the women's rights movement.

If it is appropriate to the developing dialogue, bring up and connect with social issues they may be directly dealing with, such as bullying, gender identity and equity, sexual harassment, prejudice and racism.

These teens value their unique personal responses to people, things and circumstances.

Therefore, we elicit personal connections to what they are viewing and experiencing on the tour.

Many older teens are voicing their own thoughts and views on diverse topics. Encourage this with your questions and prompts.

- *What have you seen like this before?*
- *What sorts of photographs/painting/ceramics/ gardening/sculpting do you do? Like?*
- *What appeals to you about life in this time and place?*
- *What do you think of this portrayal of a woman/man/ child?*
- *How useful do you think this object might be? Have you thought of any useful inventions yourself?*
- *Why would you suggest that a friend visit this exhibition? What might improve the exhibit for you?*

Visiting a historical museum exhibit on the Underground Railroad, students consider what it would feel like to leave everything and everyone they know to escape to an unknown place. *If you had to leave home immediately to stay safe, what would you carry with you? How would you decide who to trust?*

They talk about how it would feel to hide someone in their home. *What other examples do you know of people hiding or leaving home to stay safe?*

5 Tours with Home-school, After-school and Multi-age School Groups

Children and teens visit museums in groups other than traditional age-graded classrooms, and with a variety of interests. Home-schooled groups may have curriculum objectives and may also include children of varying ages. Some schools mix young people of different ages as part of the learning approach. Youth organizations such as Girl and Boy Scouts, 4-H, service clubs, youth centers, school clubs, and school-based child-care programs are examples of groups visiting outside of the classroom.

Home-school and after-school groups

Home-school and after-school programs have discovered that museums are excellent partners for engaging children in a variety of thinking and learning activities, through both in-person and virtual visits. Being able to see artworks, handle artifacts, examine specimens, interact with displays, and walk around historical structures help children appreciate subject matter in new and visceral ways.

The home-school teacher, often a parent, can share learning goals and links to the students' current studies if the tour is requested in advance. Art museums, zoos, science centers, natural history museums, historical sites, botanical gardens, children's centers, and others recognize their important role in educating and

> During the Lunar New Year holiday, a Girl Scout troop visited an Asian art museum to learn about traditional and contemporary art objects and celebrations. Their virtual tour promoted the Scout goal of developing global citizenship skills while having fun and started a conversation about diversity and community. Questions such as *What kinds of foods do you most enjoy during your favorite holiday?* led to lively exchanges about the importance of food and culture.

> A high school poetry club came to the museum to work on a project. Walking through the galleries with a docent, each student selected an object that would serve as the inspiration for a poem to be written after the visit. The students returned later, accompanied by their guests, and recited their poems beside their selected object.

entertaining children and providing innovative exhibits and resources for this wide audience. Many, if not most, museum websites advertise planned activities and programs for home-school and after-school groups.

Home-school and after-school groups also arrive in museums as walk-in visitors, outside regularly scheduled or reserved group programs. Often these visitors represent a mix of children of different ages with several adults. Adult participation is key to helping docents understand the interests, priorities and experiences of the children and in facilitating group engagement and cooperation. Encourage the accompanying adult(s) to:

- Share any special needs
- Stay closely connected to the group
- Use cell phones only for photographs
- Offer advice on developmentally appropriate tour adjustments
- Point out connections to topics of particular interest
- Match up children to support each other within the group
- Assist in any hands-on activities
- Guide children to restrooms and/or gift shops after the tour

In any mixed-age group of children, thoughtful, open-ended questions allow a range of developmentally appropriate responses. "What" questions, such as *What do you notice…?* and *What do you think will happen next?* encourage reflective answers rather than "correct" responses. Turn-and-talk strategies where children discuss ideas and share viewpoints also promote wider participation and understanding.

Multi-age school groups

Some schools teach children in multi-age groupings, either by intention or as necessitated by enrollment numbers. In these "vertical classrooms," children often develop keen collaboration skills as well as experience with independent learning. Some multi-age classrooms adhere closely to grade-level expectations; others blur the distinctions until students reach certain pre-determined transition points. Most often, multi-age classrooms contain two or three traditional grade levels spanning different ages.

Docents who tour multi-age school groups likely will find that younger and older students work well together, and that often older children are willing to act as guides. Students are used to partnering to pursue projects, each contributing ideas, perspectives, and skills. Turn-and-talk or pair-and-share strategies work well, with children sharing observations and learning from each other. Tour themes that resonate with class studies allow students to relate to big ideas while examining details according to their level of development and experience.

For example, seven-to-nine-year-olds exploring an oceans theme at a natural history museum might learn about whaling lore, different whale species, and environmental issues affecting whale populations. Older children may be better able to visualize and compare the huge sizes of the mammals to common objects, such as school buses.

Thinking strategies that encourage children to contribute different points of view about an object are particularly suitable to multi-age groups of young visitors.

The large, busy painted scene of Maurice Prendergast's *Docks, East Boston,* allows viewers to "step inside" and participate in the many small and ordinary events of a crowded waterfront scene.

Maurice Prendergast, "Docks, East Boston," 1900/1904, National Gallery of Art

Young people bring the painting alive with comments about what they see, hear, smell, taste and touch. They notice connections to historical elements—horses, carts, banners, storefronts. We ask: *Who is working and who is sitting? Why might there be so few women? What sounds do you hear? What clues suggest how the ships move? What might the ships be loading? Unloading? What is the weather like?* Sharing observations among children of different age groups and different levels of development enlightens the entire group.

YOUR PERSONAL NOTES

6 Special Attention

As docents, we may not know what life experiences and challenges students bring with them to the museum, such as:

- English language skills
- Visual and hearing impairments
- Different learning abilities
- Exposure to acute or chronic trauma
- Mobility issues

Here we consider specific ways to engage non-native English speakers and differently abled students, and offer all visitors a positive museum experience. To create an inclusive learning environment, one where students with and without special needs interact in activities together, we need to incorporate multimodal approaches and accommodate a range of abilities, learning styles, and skills.

Best-practice basics

What can you do to successfully engage students with special needs? Here are some general ideas to keep in mind. Many of them are sound approaches for any tour but are especially important for these young visitors.

- Everyone is different. Have a range of options so that visitors can make choices that best suit them and their needs.
- Be flexible. Follow students' interests and give opportunities for making choices.
- Be genuinely excited about what you are doing. If you are having fun, the kids will, too. Make eye contact (even if some students do not), use facial expressions and vocal color, and pay attention to the students.
- Be kind. Give positive reinforcement for engaged behavior.
- Leave more time for looking at objects and responding to them.
- Use visual and multi-sensory materials, particularly larger visuals and high-contrast materials.
- Incorporate kinesthetic or gross motor activities.
- Provide clearly defined limits and expectations for behavior.

- Repeat your instructions and clarify; check for understanding with thumbs- up confirmations.
- Build in frequent breaks. Let chaperones know it's okay to take a student away from the group for a breather if needed.
- Assign specific tasks or responsibilities to aid in focusing attention.
- Monitor your voice level and clarity. Clear voices with distinct articulation carry better than quiet ones and are more appropriate for a variety of special needs than loud ones.
- Always speak directly to a student. Don't talk down to students; treat them as you would others their age. If a student has a caregiver, interpreter or aide, address the student, not the helper.
- Some people are sensitive to lighting (very bright or dimly lit spaces), smells, touch, transitions to new spaces, and so on. Give warnings before there is a change in environment.
- Some people have difficulty making eye contact. Even if they aren't looking directly at you, talk to them because they are often listening to what you are saying.
- Welcome a variety of ways of communicating (using pictures or gestures, for example).
- It often is helpful to divide a work into parts—for example, *Let's look at the right side or top of this painting first.*

Specifics and details

Here we briefly consider five aspects of some visitors' reality that may call for your special attention during a tour. Many classrooms include students with special needs, and teachers may request or suggest specific accommodations for their students. Other times the docent may be prepared for a wide variety of learners but has no information about specific needs. Flexibility, attention and empathy are key.

English language skills

Many communities include residents for whom English

is not the primary language. Students from households where English isn't spoken may be part of a school tour. Museums and historical sites provide welcoming environments to English language learners by their very nature as low-risk places that honor and respect their diverse, lived experiences. Arts are a great equalizer in education. Regardless of native language, ability or disability, visual and performance arts are accessible to nearly all. Arts programs may be early, approachable avenues to achievement for students who are new English language learners.

Many institutions now offer tours in several languages. Docents might practice greetings and welcoming phrases for bilingual or multilingual school groups: *Ni hao; hola; konnichiwa; bonjour; namaste.*

English language learners on your tour may not be able to follow all questions and responses completely. A chance to participate in nonverbal ways is inclusive and often re-engages visitors. Be sure to provide frequent feedback and check for comprehension.

Like other special attention students, English language learners need to have a feeling of safety. They may be hesitant to speak, so it's important to wait for them to volunteer rather than shining a spotlight on them. Having them work in pairs or small groups can be an effective technique to build confidence and increase student participation.

What can we do, specifically?

- A visual schedule, map or key points of information displayed with words and pictures can help students understand what will happen on the tour.
- Quick-opinion questions can be answered with a thumbs up/thumbs down or show of hands. For example, *Using a raised hand, which do you think was harder to make, object A or object B? What do you see that makes you say that (or just, Why)?* Keep in mind that "how" is the hardest question for an English language learner to answer because of the higher-order thinking and articulation skills it requires.
- Kinetic activities get students moving. These include asking students to use their hands or bodies to make a line or shape they see in an object or to pose like a figure in the artwork. A tableau vivant, where students each take a figure or object in a work of art and pose as a group, promotes close looking as well as movement.
- Give each student three emojis: a happy face, a heart,

and a house. As students walk through the galleries, ask them to hold up the emoji for (1) an image that makes them happy; (2) an image they really connect to; and (3) an image that reminds them of home.
- Use categories. These could include people (with a stick figure emoji); things (an object emoji); and places (a travel and places emoji). Students could hold up the emoji(s) that correspond to what they see in the artwork. Follow up with the English vocabulary for these images.
- Use a reproduction of an artwork that is cut into pieces. Ask students to point to or shine a flashlight (if allowed) on their piece in the artwork. Name the object or figure.
- Ask students to translate a key word into their primary language. If looking at a landscape, point to things like a mountain, river, tree or flower and ask them how to say that in their language of origin.
- Give students a chance to participate graphically with sketches, doodles or drawings.
- Connect students' firsthand experiences and prior knowledge to the artwork. For example: *Mike says this makes him think of music and dancing. What does it make you think of? Ada says this makes her feel sad. How does it make you feel? What do you see that gives you that feeling?* Paraphrase what students say and build a conversation around earlier comments and questions to connect similarities among student responses.
- Increase wait time. English language learners may be translating your question from English to their native language, then from that language back to English for a reply. Make it easier by using the active voice: *Plants need sunlight,* not *Sunlight is needed by plants.*

Vision and hearing impairments

Teachers or chaperones frequently will request or provide accommodations for students with either vision or hearing loss. Follow their lead.

What can we do, specifically?

For blind and low vision children and teens:

- Pay attention to the location of the students relative to the object so they can fully and safely participate in activities and discussion. Children with low vision may want to get as close as possible to objects. Also, position yourself so you are not backlit, and so light is on you and not in the eyes of the students.
- Help students safely navigate the space, giving friendly directions well in advance. For example,

There is a pedestal in the middle of this room, so we we'll all move to the right. Blind children will depend on your clear, detailed descriptions to enjoy the tour.

- Use visual and multi-sensory materials, particularly larger visuals and high-contrast materials as well as textures and shapes.
- Start by giving the overall dimensions and then describe major details in a clear, concise manner. Always go from the general to the specific. Organize the description to make sense directionally: for example, top to bottom, left to right; or use clock directions, for example, at the one o'clock position.
- Provide vivid and particularized details. These might include color or texture contrasts—atmospheric effects like a billowing skirt, for instance.
- Make comments to help students understand size and scale, such as *It's three times the size of your hand.*
- Try to translate a visual experience into another sense. For example: *The robe is painted a very bright, happy yellow like the warmth of the sun on your skin. Or: This sculpture has a surface like glass.* This is a good activity for engaging other students by asking them to describe how something they see would feel, smell, taste or sound. If appropriate, find scents you can bring into the museum and share with students, such as incense for a tour that includes medieval objects.
- For low-vision students, display an image of the object on a tablet that can be enlarged to show details.
- Use music to help set the mood of an artwork. Let the group know that you will be playing music before it starts.
- After description and discussion, ask how they would feel being in that landscape or meeting that person in the portrait, or traveling in that antique convertible car.
- Be sure to give directions orally: *Follow me to the next gallery. Or I'm about to hand you a piece of stone.*

For deaf and hard-of-hearing children and teens:

- Interpreters may accompany children who use American Sign Language (ASL) and will stand near the docent to interpret. Expect that these children will carefully watch the interpreter, not the docent. Wait patiently and quietly for the interpreter to relay questions from students to you.
- Some children may lip-read or use amplification devices and provide the docent with a compatible device for the tour. Make sure that you always face the group so that students can lip-read when you are speaking. For example, gesture to objects and

their details without turning your face away from the group. If you turn, they cannot see your mouth.
- Leave more time for looking at objects and responding to them.
- Pay attention to the location of the students relative to the object so they can fully and safely participate in activities and discussion.
- Incorporate kinesthetic activities.
- Seat or place students to reduce distractions and visual stimulation.
- Ask for a variety of modes for response, not just verbal.
- Encourage raised hands; multiple voices at once can be overwhelming and distracting for those with hearing loss.

Different learning abilities

Differences in learning abilities may not be evident in a museum setting where docents usually spend only an hour or so with students. But most classrooms contain a wide range of learners, a few with educational prescriptions for extra support because of significant learning, sensory or emotional issues, a few with advanced academic skills, some with organizational challenges, some whose strengths lie in leadership, athletics or other non-academic fields. Some students learn through movement, some use their auditory senses more efficiently than their visual, and vice versa. Docents need to be aware that any tour group is likely to include students with a range of learning needs and styles.

What can we do, specifically?

- State rules clearly and positively at the beginning of the tour. Give clear directions. Tell students what they should be doing instead of what they shouldn't be doing.
- Simplify questions and directions, accept one-word answers. Set students up for success.
- Give directions in small parts, clearly, and in sequence, allowing children to process information at their own speed. Use thumbs up to acknowledge they're with you.
- For some groups, a visual schedule, map or key points of information displayed with words and pictures reinforce your message.
- Use pauses when needed for students to process information.
- Eye contact may be uncomfortable for some. A child turned away, back facing you, may be listening

carefully but avoiding visual stimulation. That child may linger at the object after the group has moved on. Try to allow different kinds of interaction during the tour.

- Offer options for creative engagement. For example, suggest a writing activity related to the tour. In addition to blank sheets of paper, provide several other choices, such as graphic organizers, lined paper, an image with room for an imaginative title or caption, directions for poetry such as haiku or free verse. Offer pencils, colored pencils, pens and markers, if allowed in an exhibition.
- Roll up a piece of paper or make "viewing tubes" from cardboard paper towel rolls to use as a telescope. This can help students focus on one part of an image at a time.
- Include pair-and-share or turn-and-talk activities to help children combine their strengths in a group setting as they discuss objects.
- Notice restless behaviors to determine whether a "fidget" object or a task might help students focus better.

Fidgets help those children who are overstimulated by their environment. Wiggle seats, manipulatives and fidgets (small hand-held objects that keep restless fingers busy, bodies relaxed, and minds focused—see figure) help those who need sensory input or who are very active.

Fidgets courtesy of the Walters Art Museum, Baltimore

Trauma

Trauma can be thought of as a "hidden" special need, for we often do not know that children may have been exposed. Field trips can be positive experiences for children affected by trauma if we offer support and understanding. We need to recognize that sometimes what we consider bad behavior may be evidence of the impact of trauma and not take it personally. What we view as disinterested or negative responses may have served a purpose at some time in the child's life. Being non-judgmental is key to a positive experience for these children.

Behavior related to acute or chronic trauma can include:

- Inability to focus due to hypervigilance or lack of sleep
- Startle response, in a constant state of fight, flight or freeze
- Emotional instability or disengagement
- Challenges with empathy
- Poor social skills, such as acting younger or older than their age
- Over- or under-controlling behavior, or a combination
- Delay in receptive or expressive language; that is, children who aren't responding may have trouble receiving, processing or generating language
- Difficulties with motor planning, fine and/or gross motor skills, and/or sensory processing

What can we do, specifically?

- Focus on the positive, as always.
- Treat behaviors as separate from the person.
- Give directions in manageable steps, allowing children to process information at their own speed.
- Provide as much detail and clarity as needed to be successful.
- Establish and follow routines for the tour:
  • After your introduction, review the tour schedule. For example: *You're going to be with me in the museum for the next hour. We're going to be on this floor, in three different rooms, or galleries.*
  • Announce transitions ahead of time and at transition time. For example: *We're going to spend another minute here…another 30 seconds here… Now it's time to move to our next object/room.*
  • If the routine needs to shift, announce it. Flexibility to adapt to the group's needs is key to a student-centric tour.

- Offer choices or options. This is a good way to provide a level of ownership and control in the tour.
- Be flexible: It's okay if a student chooses not to engage with any of the choices. It's not our job to pressure them to engage with museum objects.
- Do check-ins with the group: *Everyone okay? Thumbs up or down.*
- Always offer an "out" or way to take an emotional or physical break. Review this throughout the tour so it can be a normal adjustment. For example: *It's okay if you need to take a break. Just let me know.*
- Give children tasks to do. One task is to be the caboose or the sweep, to make sure everyone is with the group as it moves to the next stop.
- Pick your battles. If a behavior isn't hurting anyone or anything, it's probably okay to let it go. Arrange a cooling-off period if needed.

The most important things we can do are to have fun, recognize the humanity of others, exhibit empathy, and be supportive and flexible.

Mobility issues

Students on our tours may have temporary or permanent mobility issues. Students with crutches, braces, canes, wheelchairs, or scooters may come for a tour. Docents should ask teachers in advance about whether the tour group will include students with mobility issues. Recognize that mobility issues may arise at the last minute, for example, the student who breaks her leg days before the tour. Plan your tour path so that the rooms and objects you use are accessible to these students. If the tour path includes a lift to bypass a short set of stairs, be sure to alert personnel who operate the lift that you will need their help on the tour. Be flexible and prepared to use a different object or gallery if the lift is temporarily out of service.

Best practice is to keep the group together. If one student needs an accessible museum entrance, the entire group should use the same entrance. The same practice applies to use of elevators in the museum, although not stair-bypass lifts. Be prepared with information on the location of ADA-compliant restrooms. If benches are not available at tour stops, provide portable stools if the museum has them. Finally, be sure to ask the group to allow students with a scooter or wheelchair to move to the front of the group so they can see objects on the tour.

7 Candid Conversations

Museum tours often expose students to new experiences and a fuller view of cultures, histories and ideas that are unfamiliar to them or for which they have preconceived ideas and information. Sometimes this exposure raises important topics that docents and young visitors may be hesitant and even uncomfortable addressing in the context of a tour. Museums of all kinds contain objects reflecting religious beliefs, nudity and sex, race and racism, questions of gender, or death, war and violence. These subjects provide opportunities for growth and wonder. Our discussions give children permission to understand in age-appropriate and non-judgmental ways important parts of their world. As children and teens encounter new experiences in our inclusive museums, we hope they see themselves as well as others through the objects, artworks, and structures on their visits.

Docents and guides are educators and role models and can provide younger visitors positive opportunities to move beyond prejudices, misinformation and fears. So look for ways to make young visitors feel engaged and listened to as they try out new perspectives.

Religion

Museums' and cultural institutions' diverse collections may include objects created for religious and ritual use. They were made to teach and inspire awe and reverence among religious believers. There are many examples, representative of the world's many religions: ceremonial masks of the indigenous Haida people, Renaissance paintings of Christian saints, pages from the Islamic holy book, the Qur'an, bronze sculptures of the Hindu deity Shiva, cloisonné Buddhist stupas. For some students, this may be their first opportunity to learn about different religions.

Once placed in a museum, a religious object's original function and sacred nature is fundamentally changed. However, it remains tangible evidence of the religious beliefs and practices for which it was made. Many of these objects may be old, but they can represent ongoing religious practices honored by faith groups in our communities.

Many schools teach their students about diverse religions, starting in elementary classrooms. Globalization and the realities of world conflicts make developing tolerance based on understanding more critical than ever. Museums and their religious-origin objects offer students opportunities for empathy with world views that are too often distorted or maligned.

Introducing young people to objects that are expressions of unfamiliar religions, or aspects of their own religion, requires care and sensitivity. Students may come with preconceived ideas and expectations. Your tour, and the discussions you encourage, offer opportunities to model respect for the beliefs of others, grounded in fairness, accuracy, and balance.

Some how-tos:

- Remember you are teaching *about* religion, not teaching *a* religion.
- Portray beliefs and practices as their adherents understand them.
  - *Christians venerate Mary because they believe she is the mother of Jesus, who they believe is the son of God.*
  - *In Hindu belief, Shiva is both destroyer and creator of the world.*
  - *This mask, made by an artist of the Nuna people, represents a nature spirit, bridging earth and sky.*
  - *According to a Buddhist sutra, Buddha was born with these distinctive body characteristics.*
- Bring objects and their meaning into the realm of the students' experience.
  - Looking at a page from the Qur'an, ask students if they know/use any books that guide them in their beliefs and behaviors.
  - *This image of the Buddha was used by believers as a focus for meditation to reach enlightenment. Do you know someone who practices meditation?*

- *This Mesoamerican figure was the focus of appeals for a successful crop. What issues do we have today with food availability?*
- *What does "sacred" mean? What makes something "sacred" to you? What would be an example?*

- Promote empathy and the ability to see other points of view.
  - *This object was very important to the people of that time. I wonder why? Any ideas?*
  - *What do you think people from the time this was made (or now) were feeling that made this object so powerful?*
  - *There are many religions. What religions do people you know practice?*

- Discuss together how the object was made, what materials were used, and where they came from, the skills required, and how the maker might have acquired them.

- Older students can engage with religious objects to consider more complex ideas such as:
  - Religions are internally diverse.
  - Religions are dynamic, changing.
  - Religions influence and are influenced by culture.
  - Religions change as they move to different parts of the world.
  - Different religions share some common beliefs or themes.

- Looking closely together for details on religious objects can provide the avenue to explore meaning and belief.
  - *Why do you think the maker of this mask chose a butterfly?*
  - *Why do you think this statue has multiple arms?*
  - *At the time and place this was painted, dragons symbolized evil. What images do we have today of a person or group overcoming evil? Why do you think this would be important to represent in art?*

- Describing religious practices connected to objects can help visitors better understand their use. However, it is inappropriate to engage students in imitative practices (for example, praying positions, processionals, crossing oneself). Such activity is insensitive to the believers and raises concerns among teachers and families that we may be encouraging visitors to practice a different religion. Instead, you might show a video or picture of an object being used by believers (for example, puja in India).

- Try to use language that does not imply religious value: Krishna, not Lord Krishna; Jesus, not Christ.

First graders were encouraged to circle the large bronze statue of Nandi, the Hindu sacred bull. At the back of the sculpture Nandi's male genitals are accurately displayed. The children start to giggle and whisper. You might say, *So, is this a male or a female? How do you know? You can see the testicles. This tells us that Nandi is a bull, the general name for this male animal.*

"Nandi," India, 12th century, Freer Gallery of Art, Smithsonian Institution, Washington, D.C.: Purchase – Charles Lang Freer Endowment, F1985.30

Nudity, sex and gender

Museums may have objects, paintings and artifacts showing human nudity, animal sexual anatomy, relationships between men and women, gender identity, and suggestive or even explicit representations of sexual activity. Zoo animals are often not shy in front of visitors. You might choose not to include a certain item in your tour, but on entering a gallery kids will look around and see what is there. Talking about nudity, sex, gender and relationships may not be a priority on a tour. But these topics are much on the minds of young visitors, and they will have reactions, comments, opinions and questions. No need to avoid them. The response you make and the information you provide will vary depending on the age of the visitors, but there are some general good-practice guidelines.

- Speak honestly and accurately about what they are seeing/is happening. Use real words for body parts and not nicknames.

Sometimes nakedness is part of the story. *Why do you think this person is shown with no clothes? What's happening in the story? How would it be different if the person were dressed?*

- Older students benefit from an opportunity to talk about their feelings, attitudes and values concerning sex, sexual relationships and gender fluidity and identity.
  - Ancient Greek statues of male athletes are often nude. Explain that this is how Greek athletes competed. This is an opportunity to ask if the group includes any athletes and how they might feel competing this way. A painting or a statue showing nudity can be an opportunity to discuss their views concerning dress and nudity in our society and cultural differences over time and in various places. Remember their point of view may be different from your own.
  - Ancient Greeks believed a beautiful male or female body was the closest humans come to being like the gods. The best way to see that beauty was without clothes. In the Renaissance, artists followed the example of ancient Greece and made many statues and paintings of people without clothes.
  - *This portrait shows her at fifteen, just as she is to be married. What age is a good one to marry, do you think? Why? Why might it have been common to marry at fifteen at the time this was made?*
  - Some religious figures are portrayed as either a man or a woman in different images or with an ambiguous face and body. *What does that suggest about the society's thinking? Does it make a difference whether we see this figure as a man or a woman or if we can't figure out which it is?*
- Objects may show or imply sexual violence and historical attitudes about gender and power.
  - The 12th-century painted ceramic cup tells a story from the Persian epic *Shahnameh* when a king renounces and banishes his daughter because she has fallen in love with an enemy.
  - An image of Medusa, a Siren, or a Greek sphinx raises the issue of the patriarchal nature of Ancient Greece and the portrayal of strong women as monsters.
- Sexual harassment – what constitutes positive relationships? How men and women should treat each other is a vital part of discussions today.
- Your responses can model that noticing and talking about nudity and sex in a responsible way is healthy and constructive. In the same way, conversations

that lead to more complex versus simplistic ideas about gender, gender differences and gender identity promote tolerance and inclusiveness.

Race/racism/cultural differences

A museum visit can expose young people to artifacts, artistic expressions, ideas and beliefs that come from diverse cultures. "Culture" in this sense broadly includes race and ethnicity, religion, age and physical or mental differences. Our visitors self-identify with a variety of cultures, as do docents. We bring our own cultural world views to the museum visit, influencing our responses to what we see and hear. This provides opportunities to expand horizons and enrich our knowledge of a wider world. It also, at times, presents visitors and us with "others," that is, people who are perceived as not like ourselves.

American society is confronting long-standing systemic racial injustice and inequities. Many museums have taken stands against racism and are working to incorporate equity and inclusion in every aspect of their programing.

Our student visitors are often passionate participants in conversations and activities dealing with these issues— on all sides. This is particularly challenging when young people voice beliefs and attitudes reflective of assumptions, stereotypes, prejudice and occasionally, profound misunderstandings. Our diverse young visitors might experience a deeply felt response to a museum object that reflects their own community or cultural heritage. This can differ from our curatorial-based perspective.

We strive to be audience-centered museums, and that means audience contributions matter. Our young visitors bring personal knowledge and life experience with them to the museum. Our task is to respect what these visitors bring.

We want to create an encouraging environment for dialogue and participation, where visitors can share views and experiences reflecting their own and other cultures. The goal is to create dialogue and conversation that lead to deepening knowledge, understanding and empathy. What to do?

- Accept that you bring your own explicit and implicit biases to the tour and work to be aware of them. Each of us has history and experiences that shape our sense of "the truth."

- Be non-judgmental in your response to student comments. Ask the student to say more about what is meant or how they came to that understanding. Ask if others in the group have different ideas or experiences. Use and model respectful responding, such as: *I agree with part of what Joe said, and I also think that…* Or, *I get that you're uncomfortable...*
- Ask open-ended questions to the whole group, with an emphasis on *What do you think/feel about what we are looking at?* that allows you to ask for others to comment. Remember each student's response is their personal truth. Hearing from others promotes empathy and perspective-taking.
- Present other viewpoints and other "truths," including that of the curators, historical record, and other sources. Ask for reactions and discussion of this information. Resist the temptation to lecture or to insist on what is "correct," but do state what your own understanding is.
- Encourage students to think about all the stories an object has witnessed over time and what hands have touched it over time.
- Create safety to express oneself so that students can hear and learn from each other.
- Avoid singling out a student who may belong to the culture represented to comment and explain.
- Respond to students who make derogatory statements about another culture by saying that this is hurtful and not respectful. Then reach for the personal experience or attitude that lies behind it. *That is a hurtful statement. What has been your experience with X?* Reach for empathy. *If you were a person from [culture X], what do you think it would feel like to hear that?*

Examples:

- An artwork shows people dressed in tattered and dirty clothing and a student says, "Those are lazy poor people just hanging out." Ask a question you genuinely want to know the answer to. *Where would you try to get help if your family were facing hard times?*
- At an historical house museum, the docent talks about its Mexican family owners. A child responds, "Mexicans used to own this place? I thought they only worked here." The docent talks about the different nationalities of people who have lived in the area that once was a part of Mexico.
- At another museum, a 19th-century painting includes a Black person. A child says, "That must be a slave." The docent explains about free African-Americans at the time.

George Bellows, "The Lone Tenement," 1909, National Gallery of Art

- *Has there been a time when you were accused of something you didn't do?*
- *Do you have friends or know people who are different from you? In what way?*

War, violence and death

Images and implements of war and violence can be upsetting, particularly for children and teens who have experienced trauma. They might question why these things are in a museum and whether medieval crossbows, swords, ceremonial knives and gilded muskets might be used to attack them while they are in the museum. Paintings showing a battle or the suffering of a religious figure can evoke scenes of violence children may have seen or discussions they may have had at school or at home. Images of people killed by police are painted on billboards and violence is shown on cell phone videos and widely shared on social media. Young people have passionate views about these happenings, which may be brought to the fore as they encounter museum objects, making a powerful connection to their own lives.

One way to approach this is to focus on the objects themselves:

- *What do you notice about the objects?*
- *Why do you think the museum might have these objects?*
- *Who might have made them and what skills would have been needed?*
- *What other objects could people with these skills have made?*
- *Who would have used them?*

- *How have changes in technology affected objects like these?*
- *What do we have today that is similar to these objects?*

Objects, artifacts and works of art are all a reflection of the people and time period in which they were created and used. *How does our view of these objects in a museum differ from the way the people who made and used them might have seen them? What do you think the people who made and used these objects would feel about having them in a museum today?*

Battle scenes are common images in many museums. One approach is to talk about war as a way that groups of people or countries try to resolve their differences or gain advantage over each other. Because conflict has always been a part of human life, artists in many different eras and places have represented battles and fight scenes. In a world with conflict, artists use their abilities to find meaning out of pain. Seeing the images can teach us about ourselves and help us understand some of the universal elements of the human condition.

Another approach is to talk about images telling a story about a real or imagined event. *Why do you think the artist thought it was important to make a record of this event? Who are the characters? What character traits might the scene be highlighting, such as courage, perseverance or cowardice?*

A similar approach can be taken to images of death. Some children may have experienced the death of a pet, a relative, a neighbor or a friend. Many are aware of the deaths that have happened from violence and the COVID-19 pandemic. A child visiting a house museum asks, "Did anyone die in this house?" Children today may assume that people always died in a hospital. Objects and images in a museum can help students understand how people from different times and places made sense of death and what rituals they performed when someone died. An image of a dead person might also be part of a story, including a religious story such as Jesus on a cross.

In all these conversations, let students know that it's okay to find some topics tough, and it's okay to talk about them. Ask why an object is scary for a student, if that's what they expressed. Students who are frightened by a mummy, for example, may be worried that it's going to come to life and attack them—a good opportunity to explain Egyptian beliefs about the afterlife. Observe the behavior and tone of voice of a student expressing concern to determine which direction the conversation should take.

_____

_____

_____

_____

_____

_____

_____

_____

_____

_____

_____

_____

_____

_____

_____

_____

_____

_____

_____

_____

_____

_____

8 Challenging Behaviors

We begin our tours by welcoming young people to the museum warmly and personally and describing ways to make the visit a success. As with any tour, however, some school-age visitors may act in ways that challenge our ability to stay on track. The best-planned tours and most enthusiastic docents/guides, even experienced ones, acknowledge certain challenging situations. We learn from each other some of the strategies and routines that help engage a variety of students and recognize that any preconceived ideas of "good museum behavior" need to be reexamined.

The best strategies are proactive. We encourage behaviors and expectations that promote curiosity, fun and connections. We anticipate normal differences among young people, their learning styles, and attention spans. We describe to chaperones and students the kinds of behaviors that ensure a successful museum experience. We avoid negative body language or signs of disapproval. Children who need loving connection the most will often ask for it in the most unloving ways. We need to see past these outward behaviors to the need within.

We stress that teachers and adult chaperones can be docents' allies in engaging students during a museum tour. Start with communication before the visit, continue to interact with the adults upon arrival with quick conferences about changes or special needs, and maintain contact with the adults during the tour. They usually know the students best. If appropriate, request their assistance in offering attention and support to specific individuals during the tour.

Here are some common challenging behaviors and suggestions regarding what to do about them.

The challenges

Quiet ones

Most children and teens in a tour group have a variety of learning styles and personalities. But occasionally a group or an individual seems unusually quiet—reserved, shy or even disinterested. Most of us have led at least one tour where few students answered questions or offered comments. What to do? First, a quick checklist might help:

- Can I be seen and my voice heard by everyone?
- Am I using touring strategies that invite students to talk with one another, rather than speak in front of the whole group?
- Have I tried a question or task that invites each member of the group to respond? For example: *If you could send a postcard or an image of one object we've seen today to a family member/friend, which one would it be? What would it say about the object?* Then give all a chance to share within the group.
- Are my questions open-ended enough to encourage a variety of responses rather than "right answers"?
- Have I provided non-verbal ways to participate in the tour, such as "thumbs up," movement activities, writing or sketching, or examining hands-on materials? Quiet young people may be engaged but prefer not to speak.
- Am I responding to brief comments by paraphrasing the remarks and using *Yes, and...* to encourage further discussion?

Here are strategies that can be useful:

- At the beginning of the tour, ask all the students to introduce themselves, which can sometimes break the ice. Consider telling teens the personal pronouns you prefer to use. This can help create a sense of inclusion so that non-binary identity students feel safe and respected.
- Use "pair and share" or "turn and talk" to generate comments and thoughts. Or ask students to find a partner or a small group and work on a task together, then report back to the group. Often students will talk to each other even if they hesitate to speak in the larger group.
- Let students know there are no right or wrong answers to your questions (and make sure that is

true). Your time together is one of discovery.

- Incorporate movement for younger students. Moving together helps groups to bond, which may make it easier for students to feel comfortable talking.
- Use a question that requires a thumbs up/down response: *How many of you would like to have more than two hands, like this statue of Ganesha? Then follow up: How many hands would you like to have? What would you do with extra hands?*
- If only one or two students are quiet, give them a special task that will let them participate without speaking. One example: *Would you like to be the first to hold this piece of jade and pass it to your classmate?*

Too often docents feel a tour hasn't been successful because visitors haven't been uniformly talkative. But in *Quiet: The Power of Introverts in a World That Can't Stop Talking*, Susan Cain reminds us that introverts "... listen more than they talk, think before they speak..." and "...have mighty powers of concentration." If your quiet students have been attentive and engaged and participate in non-verbal ways, you can count your tour just right for them.

Talkers
On the other end of the spectrum, the assertive talker replies to every question and talks at length. Her hand is up first, while everyone else is still thinking about the question. Or many in the group talk at the same time, interrupting or shouting out comments without listening to one another. While we value enthusiasm, this behavior makes it hard for all students to participate and for the docent to facilitate the conversation. Talkative students, whether an individual or a group, may thrive on the stimulation of new discoveries and opportunities to engage not only with objects but with peers and adults. Some classroom limits have been removed, and tendencies toward sociability and assertiveness emerge in the new setting. Here are some suggestions:

- Reinforce positive behaviors such as taking turns and waiting for others to finish speaking. Remind students to raise their hands: *Manuel, I'm calling on you because you're raising your hand. Great job raising your hand.* Or if several are responding at once: *I hear some interesting points and would like to know more about your thoughts. Remember we agreed that each of you would raise your hand before you talk. I promise to call on you.*
- Acknowledge classmates' contributions. Some schools

routinely encourage students to silently wiggle "thumbs up" when in agreement with a classmate's comments rather than add on additional remarks.
- Incorporate a slow-looking activity, as described in Chapter One. Or use a brief clarifying exercise: *With lowered eyes, let's take deep, calm breaths for one minute before we move on to the next object.*
- Ask the group if anyone who hasn't had a chance to talk would like to share their comments. *Who hasn't had airtime who would like to comment?*
- One museum uses the phrase, "Take space; make space." *If you usually are quiet, take some space to give your opinion. If you usually participate actively, make space for others to talk.*
- Pair the talker with a quieter student for pair-and-share activities.
- Use a group activity, such as the See-Think-Wonder routine with pencils and stickies on clipboards, to give students a chance to participate individually and quietly.

Wanderers
Our youngest students may find their attention wandering and let their feet follow. Older children and teens may spot a fascinating object and want to know more. Teens may want to assert their autonomy and self-direction. Some young visitors may find it difficult to stay with the group (see Chapter Six). Whatever is behind this wandering, visitors in a docent-led tour need both structure and flexibility. The balance will shift one way or the other according to the group and its needs. What to do? A few ideas:

- Use guided discovery. Give students a goal, something to find in a gallery. *Spend a few minutes looking at one object that fascinates you and that you'd like to tell a friend or family member about. Zoom in and look closely at details, then zoom out and see the whole object. Repeat. How will you describe your object? We'll gather in _____ minutes.* Give students a finish-up signal before you ask them to gather. *Who would like to share their discovery?*
- Offer options. Build a sense of participation by offering choices about what students see or the order of the objects in a tour. *We're about to enter the reptile house. Would you like to start with the Burmese rock python or the Aldabra tortoise?*
- Connect to student interests. One student seems particularly curious about an object not on your tour. Use that interest as a link back to your theme. *Jacob Lawrence paintings seem to focus on human*

dignity and freedom. Look how the one you've noticed, featuring Harriet Tubman, connects to these migration paintings. What do you think?

- Use positive reinforcement. *I must stop and tell you how much I appreciate how hard you're listening and looking. I can see you are really thinking about this artwork and have some questions.*

- Alert students that a transition is about to happen. *In two minutes, we're going to move from this room to another room...In another minute, we're going to move to the door...It's time now for us to move to another room.*

Successfully engaging your visitors in the tour process is the best solution to wandering attention and behavior. The ideas presented here are bedrock approaches for any tour you will have.

Touchers

Some museum objects seem to invite touching, to slide along the cool surface of a Chinese ceramic or to bang on the glass of the Great Ape House. Sometimes a hands-on reproduction is available to pass around, but one museum rule prevails above most others: No Touching! Children and teens need to hear this rule at the beginning of the tour and be reminded as needed. Hands-on materials, when available, are helpful, but visitors must hear a version of "hands-off" whenever temptation arises. What to do when a visitor is tempted to touch? Some ideas:

- Use body measures. *Stretch your arms out in front of you, elbows straight, careful not to touch a classmate. Now to one side. That's how far away you should be from a museum object.* Even when we encourage students to move around a freestanding object to see all angles, they may need reminders to keep an arm's distance away.

- Use a temporary divider. *I'm placing my scarf/muffler on the floor as a reminder to stay this far away from the work of art. It's an oil painting without glass to protect the surface, so we need to be extra careful to keep a safe distance.*

- Reinforce positive behavior by catching them at being good. *Alex, you've really figured out what to do with your hands in a museum. Thank you for keeping them in your pocket and not touching.*

- Use the floor. Some museums have carpet squares or small, portable stools for children, larger ones for teens and adults. They not only provide structured seating and protection for objects, but also a means

for visitors to sit comfortably, relax and look closely all at once. However, the objects must be large enough or low enough to provide easy viewing.

Jokesters and other distractions

Teachers or adult chaperones are your best allies when children or teens act inappropriately in a museum setting, showing excessive or continuous silliness, pranking, arguing, taunting, romantic gestures, or variations that cause discomfort to classmates and adults. Make clear, firmly and respectfully, that the specific behavior is inappropriate in the museum and draw in one or more adults with the group to reinforce the message. Many students will adjust immediately. A few may need a time away from the tour to refocus. Some examples of what you might say:

- *That comment to your classmate is disrespectful and inappropriate. Just as at school, you may not use those words here in the museum.*

- *A good way to get control of the giggles is to move away from your classmates and refocus on your own curiosity about this object. What was it that struck you as funny about this piece?* It is not uncommon for the whole group to get the giggles with certain objects. *OK, ten seconds to let the giggles out and then let's focus here.*

- *Your argument seems unrelated to our museum tour, am I right? As we continue our conversation about this object, please set aside your disagreement. Perhaps the time here will give you a chance to reflect on ways to come to a resolution.*

- *I'm distracted by your affectionate behavior, and I think others may be too. I hope you'll tune back into our discussion.*

If the group or enough of the members are not responding to your efforts to refocus, move the students off to the side or to a corner. Talk together about respect, collaboration and the opportunity to explore ideas outside the classroom. You might say: *I'm concerned that this isn't working. Tell me how I can make this tour more comfortable for all of us.* If nothing else works, think about taking students to a place in the museum where they can be boisterous.

Adults accompanying the tour

We stress that teachers and accompanying adult chaperones are the docent's allies during the tour. Clarifying expectations before the tour begins is the best strategy. You are counting on their help and support with the tour. However, occasionally you will encounter challenging adult behaviors. Adults, happy to have the docent managing the group, may ignore the tour, wander off to look on their own, or talk to each other or on the phone. Or, in the opposite case, chaperones, enthusiastic and involved, may ask many questions or comment frequently, crowding out the students. Here are suggestions:

- As you welcome your group to the museum, tell chaperones they are part of your team, you're grateful to have them along, and their active participation helps you do your job. *When we move, I'll be at the front, and if you sweep up stragglers from the back, we'll be able to stay together as a team.* Young children might visualize the analogy of a sandwich: *I'm a piece of bread, you're the peanut butter and jelly, and your teacher is the other slice. Let's stick together!*
- Ask students to thank the chaperones for coming on the field trip today.
- Ask the chaperones for assistance during the tour, not just with behavior challenges, but also with activities such as passing out hands-on materials and returning them to the docent.
- For the too-talkative adult, re-direct attention to the students. *That is a great question/comment. Let's see what the students think about it.* Or turning to the students: *What are your thoughts about that comment?*

Six key ideas to remember in dealing with challenging behavior:

1. **Composure:** Smile, take a breath, and relax. We can only control how we react to students in our care, not how they react. Spend some quiet time before students arrive to calm and center ourselves and practice being flexible. Students pick up on our emotional state. We can only provide emotional safety for students when we ourselves are emotionally safe.

2. **Choices:** *Would you like to look at this piece or this other one first?* Using students' interests builds community.

3. **Encouragement:** To create community conversation, build caring and helpfulness.

4. **Positive intent:** Focus on what we want/want more of; be willing to see the best in others, looking past the behavior of the moment to see the essence of the person and the underlying need the behavior demonstrates.

5. **Empathy:** Supportive, non-judgmental acceptance works. Keep calm, describe the behavior we see without judgment, name it, and ask for what we do want.

6. **Learn from experience:** Let your missteps be "oopses" to learn from rather than weights to bear.

Final points

Challenging behaviors in a museum or historical site are not about the docent or the visit. During our brief time with students, we encourage, surprise, affirm and inform, among other ways to promote curiosity and connection, but we do not discipline or act as negative authority figures. Our toolboxes contain plenty of empathy, strategies, and non-judgmental ways to inspire collaboration and deep thinking among our diverse young visitors. Not every student will respond in the same way, but our respect for them and our pleasure in welcoming them into our institutions should be clear.

YOUR PERSONAL NOTES

_____

_____

_____

_____

_____

9 Live Virtual Tours

Things are changing for museums and docents/ guides. Museums are increasing their digital presence to attract new audiences, both adult and school-aged, and to craft opportunities for sharing their collections in new ways. Docent-led tours can be a vital part of this expansion **if we think digitally**. There are many potential avenues for docents and guides to interact virtually with museum audiences. Here we discuss one – synchronous (live, in real time), interactive virtual tours. A shift in approach and a step-by-step process to foster competence and confidence are the keys to giving successful and rewarding virtual tours.

For many docents, lack of familiarity with some of the necessary technology for live online touring presents a challenge. On the other hand, we are experiencing more and more aspects of a digital life. We are always delighted to welcome groups to our museums, but we know that virtual touring, in a variety of forms, is here to stay. With training, practice and plenty of help, docents and guides can become successful virtual tour leaders.

Virtual touring and the technology to support it are relatively new and evolving. Schools are adapting, with many planning to offer remote learning to some students permanently. Many classrooms are equipped with the technology to support virtual experiences of various kinds, and teachers are finding new and flexible resources to support learning goals. Museums that offer virtual tours for school-aged groups find them popular and much in demand. Different models of docent-led tours are emerging. What we discuss here is based on several models for children and teens. With time and experience, the processes will adapt and change and be handled differently by different museums.

Key components of a live virtual tour
Remember tour basics
A live, online tour for children and teens is still a tour for young people. Everything presented in the earlier chapters—strategies and techniques for making tours engaging and interactive for audiences of different ages—applies to virtual tours. There are challenges and unique opportunities, but the bottom line is still fundamental good touring technique.

Plan with care. All the basics outlined in Chapter One—developing a tour theme with supporting objects/stops, choosing the most relevant content, and building in strategies and techniques for an engaging experience—are the same as for any in-person tour. Advance collaboration with a teacher or adult leader, important for all tours, is essential for handling technological issues and their management. This is discussed in more detail below.

Tour technology
The technological demands of live online tours with groups of students may mean more staff involvement in the tour process than is generally the case with in-person docent/guide-led tours. Live virtual tours require familiarity with the technology infrastructure by all users: the classroom teacher, individual students, docents/guides, and supporting museum staff regardless of location. At this writing, many schools are using Zoom as their platform. Basic comfort and practice with this program, or others, and its smooth interface with the docent's chosen device (desktop, laptop, tablet, PC or iOS) is essential.

The second technological requirement, in many instances, is a working ability to construct a slide presentation in PowerPoint or some other presentation program. A presentation program allows docents to present images from their collections with close-up enhancement of details, and if relevant and useful, embedded supplementary video and audio material from nearly endless web resources. As museums re-open, docent virtual tours also may be live videos in front of the objects on display or may use pre-recorded videos of these objects with live docent-led discussion.

But, as we discuss in "Opportunities and advantages" below, there is potential richness in constructing a tour that can draw on your entire museum collection, whether objects are currently displayed or not. And, unlike videotaping in the museum itself, tour construction using presentation program slides can be undertaken by the docent independently.

Training and practice opportunities in Zoom and PowerPoint or other presentation programs must be provided before your museum embarks on docent/guide-led virtual tours. Some docents may be comfortable and even expert in the technology and software, and can mentor and assist others; however, staff support and expertise are likely to be critical.

Collaboration

Live virtual touring depends on close collaboration with the requesting/sponsoring teacher or adult. The choice of tour, goals for visitors, any connections to concurrent studies, and the tour date and timing are all figured out in collaboration between museum staff and/or docents and the teacher/adult. Beyond this typical exchange, the teacher/adult will need to clarify the specific technology set-up for the classroom/group. Will all students be in the classroom or signing in remotely, or both? If in the classroom, will students have their own devices to view the tour or use one large screen? How will tour conversation, questions and comments be handled? Will hands be raised? Will the Zoom chat feature be used? Teachers will advise about the best approach.

Typically, the student group, whether each on a remote device or together in a classroom, is too large for everyone's image or name to display on the docent's screen. The teacher/adult becomes a critical partner to help the flow of discussion as the tour progresses and ensure that all have a chance to be recognized.

The best practice for virtual touring uses a partnership, either between docents or with docent and staff. Working in tandem, one docent is "lead" and conducts the tour. The other docent or staff member is the "facilitator," monitoring and assisting with the technology, including Zoom procedures and the slide presentation, and often assisting with student-docent exchanges. If multiple groups are involved for the same tour, a "team" for each group is used. Dry runs of the tour involving the docent and the facilitator are useful for ironing out technical issues, practice with timing,

and agreeing on the tour process.

Encourage docents who may be reluctant to give virtual touring a try by inviting them to join a tour rehearsal (all participants are on Zoom), or to shadow an actual tour as a silent Zoom member. Once the online tour presentation is constructed, this can be shared and used by different docents. Likewise, the tour talking points, template, or if used, actual script can be shared.

Tour interaction

A virtual tour is touring at a distance. The immediate connection with your visitors of an in-person warm greeting and welcoming eye-contact is missing. Getting your visitors' attention, "warming up the group," is important. Try to pique curiosity and interest with a question or appeal that connects to your tour theme. *What is your favorite celebration? Who has flown on an airplane? How was it? Who has visited... before?*

Presentation and delivery matter. Your "presence" is limited to a small screen, eliminating some of the subtlety of in-person verbal and non-verbal communication, while at the same time amplifying the impact of facial expression and vocal tone. Practice in front of the camera so you are aware of how you look to the viewer. Be sure your face and shoulders will be seen. Maintain eye contact. Slowing down your delivery and careful use of pauses will help your viewers absorb and think about what you say and ask. Give plenty of time for responses.

The tour should be engaging, using many of the same techniques discussed for in-person tours. Resist the urge to talk too much. Instead encourage lots of close looking. The images you have chosen can be magnified to provide details that may not be easily seen in the museum. Let your audience point out all that they see and what they think about it. Tell the teacher ahead of time that you want to have the kids sketch, so they will need pencil and paper. Have them stand up and move in response to an object at some point. Use questions and prompts to get reactions and ideas, using the teacher/adult or your partner/facilitator to call on students to speak. If the students have their own devices, you can use interactive features of Zoom—chat, raised hands, and polls—to encourage participation and group sharing other than talking.

Challenges

Virtual tours are different. Tours with children and teens may have more single responses and less conversational exchange. Tours often are requested for an entire classroom, making for a greater docent-visitor ratio than we typically provide at the museum. There is a loss of scale for the objects we are examining, and a screen image, no matter how clear, does not have the same impact as viewing the object in person. When our young visitors are viewing the tour remotely, there can be distractions and internet problems that interfere with engagement and enjoyment.

The technology does not always work as intended, even for the most expert user. This may be the case for the docent working at home or for the teacher and students in the classroom. Flexibility and patience are key, just as with our in-person tours. Amplifying students' voices so they can be heard clearly often is challenging. The teacher or your partner/facilitator may paraphrase or repeat comments or questions, but some spontaneity inevitably is lost.

All that being so, there are many reasons to add virtual touring to our repertoire.

Opportunities and advantages

Museums and their docents are enthusiastic about the new dimensions virtual touring bring to programming. New and diverse audiences from around the world now have access to what the museum offers, either through video or images, if the collection is digitized. Schools that were unable to arrange in-person tours because of distance, transportation obstacles, lack of resources, or time now find they can arrange a tour.

In constructing a tour, you can choose from the entire museum collection, not just what is on view. You can easily juxtapose images of objects that might not be shown together and make comparisons with distant or unavailable works that have images online.

PowerPoint supplies useful tools to enhance viewing. The magnifying tool allows careful inspection of details, with no labels to tell eager readers what they are seeing. Once you learn, it is simple to embed supplementary material from the web such as video, animation, music and contextual photos and maps that enliven your presentation. When incorporating material from the web, be cognizant of copyright and provide appropriate citations.

And, not least of all, virtual tours mean more viewing, less time on the bus, or time traveling the hallways and moving around the museum/historical site. There are no other tours to bump into or work around. Virtual touring is here to stay.

YOUR PERSONAL NOTES

Resources

Introduction

https://www.utoledo.edu/honors/visual-literacy/

Chapter One: Basics

Theory into Practice: The Visual Thinking Strategies, by Philip Yenawine, Presented at the conference of Aesthetic and Art Education: a Transdisciplinary Approach, 1999.

"The Art of Slow Looking in the Classroom"
https://www.gse.harvard.edu/news/uk/20/01/art-slow-looking-classroom

"The Art of Slow Looking in the Museum"
https://www.nytimes.com/2014/10/12/travel/the-art-of-slowing-down-in-a-museum/html

Tishman, Shari. (2017) *Slow Looking: The Art and Practice of Learning Through Observation*. Harvard Graduate School of Education
https://www.jstor.org/stable/40283907?seq=4#metadata_info_tab_contents

Ciasnocha, Danuta, et al. "The Power of Storytelling: An Interview with Mari-Louise Olsson, the Executive Director of the Museum of Mölndal." *The Journal of Museum Education*, vol. 31, no. 1, 2006, pp. 63–69. JSTOR, www.jstor.org/stable/40283907. Accessed 11 Nov. 2020.

"Dwelling in Possibility." Author(s): Hilary Iris Lowe Source: *The Public Historian* , Vol. 37, No. 2 (May 2015), pp. 42-60 Published by: University of California Press on behalf of the National Council on Public History Stable URL:
https://www.jstor.org/stable/10.1525/tph.2015.37.2.42

"Can You Describe the Experience?" Patrick Ryan and Donna Schatt *Storytelling, Self, Society*, Vol. 10, No. 2 (Fall 2014), pp. 131-155, Wayne State University Press Stable
https://www.jstor.org/stable/10.13110/storselfsoci.10.2.0131

"Constructing a Cultural Context through Museum Storytelling." Margaret DiBlasio and Raymond DiBlasio. *Roundtable Reports* , Spring, 1983, Vol. 8, No. 3 (Spring, 1983), pp. 7-9, Taylor & Francis, Ltd.
https://www.jstor.org/stable/40478567

Claire Bown, The Art Engager podcast, 2021
"This podcast is here to help educators, guides and creatives engage their audiences with art, objects, and ideas. Each week I'll be sharing a variety of easy-to-learn flexible techniques and tools to help you create participant-centered experiences that bring art and ideas to life."
www.thinkingmuseum.com/podcast

Chapter Three: Tours with Younger Visitors

Sarah Erdman. "Creating Meaningful Partnerships with Museums." *Young Children*, March 2016

Kelly O. Finnerty (2005) "Celebrating the Creativity of the Young Child," *Journal of Museum Education*, 30:1, 9-13, DOI: 10.1080/10598650.2005.11510512

Pamela Krakowski (2012) "Museum Superheroes." *Journal of Museum Education*, 37:1, 49-58, DOI:10.1080/105986 50.2012.11510717

Emily Erwin-McGuire, Kelly Tieger and Kate Williamson. "How Can Museum Educators Work with Chaperones." *Museum*, November-December, 2015

Pamela Duncan, *Warthogs Paint*, illus Henry Cole, 2001

Ellen Galinsky. *Mind in the Making*. Harper Collins Publishers. 2010

Veronica Boix-Mansilla@VBoixMansilla, Chair, Future of Learning Institute HGSE

Chapter Four: Tours with Teens

"A Training Program for Stepping up Effective Docent Engagement with Youth, " McNay Art Museum and Texas State Art Museum-San Marcos, Symposium breakout session, San Francisco, 2013. https://www.nationaldocents.org/presentations-and-discussions/breakout-sessions/school-touring/a-training-program-for-stepping-up-effective-docent-engagement-with-youth-2013-sf

Making Thinking Visible: How to Promote Engagement, Understanding, and Independence for All Learners by Ron Ritchhart, Mark Church, and Karin Morrison. Jossey-Bass, 2011.

The Power of Making Thinking Visible: Practices to Engage and Empower All Learners by Ron Ritchhart and Mark Church. Wiley, 2020.

McNeely and Blanchard, "The Teen Years Explained." Available as a PDF/CDC from the following link: https://books.google.com/books?hl=en&lr=&id=Vjn7E0OD1hUC&oi=fnd&pg=PP3&dq=McNeely+and+Blanchard&ots=86F3yI_c_a&sig=5kfbdzeqWiBEjO50ZjNgwYBLkHw

Chapter Five: Tours with Home-school, After-school, and Multi-age School Groups

www.learninglab.si.edu

www.beyondthechalkboard.org

https://www.pandiapress.com/homeschool-using-museums

https://thewalters.org/experience/programs/families/homeschool/

https://www.cincymuseum.org/educators/homeschool/

Chapter Six: Special Attention

https://www.nationaldocents.org/presentations-and-discussions/breakout-sessions/touring-specialty-populations/multisensory-tours-for-visually-impaired

https://medium.com/viewfinder-reflecting-on-museum-education/good-teaching-is-good-teaching-english-learners-and-museums-74270adeb537

English Language Learners in the Science Classroom Author(s): Felicia Lincoln and Caroline Beller Source: Science Scope, Vol. 28, No. 1, Teacher's Toolbox (SEPTEMBER 2004), pp. 28-31 Published by: National Science Teachers Association Stable URL: https://www.jstor.org/stable/43179260

Chapter Seven: Candid Conversations

Georgetown University Berkeley Center for Religion, Peace and World Affairs.
https://berkleycenter.georgetown.edu/

University of North Carolina Chapel Hill, Ackland Art Museum, "Five Faith Project."
https://ackland.org/five-faiths-project/

Mayo Clinic. "Healthy Lifestyle: Sexual Health."
https://www.mayoclinic.org/healthy-lifestyle/sexual-health/in-depth/sex-education/art-20044034

Smithsonian National Museum of African American History and Culture, "Talking about Race."
https://nmaahc.si.edu/learn/talking-about-race

International Coalition of Sites of Conscience.
https://www.sitesofconscience.org/en/home/

Chapter Eight: Challenging Behavior

"Tried and True Strategies for Promoting Positive Behavior During Tours," Des Moines Art Center, Symposium breakout session, Montreal, 2017.
https://www.nationaldocents.org/presentations-and-discussions/breakout-sessions/school-touring/strategies-for-promoting-positive-behavior

Conscious Discipline, a program of evidence-based programs and practices, recognized by the Substance Abuse and Mental Health Administration's National Registry of Evidence-based Programs and Practices (NREPP), which promotes the adoption of scientifically established behavioral health interventions.
https://consciousdiscipline.com/

General

For past NDS Symposium breakout sessions on school tours:
https://www.nationaldocents.org/presentations-and-discussions/breakout-sessions/school-touring

National Core Arts Standards.
https://www.nationalartsstandards.org

Minneapolis Institute of Art, "Tour Toolkit: Developing an Inclusive Tour," Tour Toolkit (artsmia.github.io)

Acknowledgments

We received suggestions and help from many individuals as we wrote the handbook. In that sense it is the product of multiple voices and hands. Sharon Edlow, docent at the Walters Art Museum, provided material for the section on tours with our youngest visitors. Docents Aggie Brenneman (San Francisco Asian Art Museum), Carol Gage (Kreeger Museum), Lola Rizkallah (Rancho Los Alamitos), Pamela Selden (Smithsonian National Museum of Natural History), Dena Watson-Lamprey (Oakland Museum of California), and staff members Margaret Yee (San Francisco Asian Art Museum) and Hillary Rothberg (Tudor Place Historical Home and Garden) offered examples from tours and insightful approaches to both in-person and virtual touring with young audiences. Heather Marek, Phoenix Art Museum, whose presentation at NDS 2019, "Conscious Conflict Management: Transforming Discipline Issues into Teaching Moments," was helpful for Chapter 8. For assistance with sensitive and accurate information concerning students with vision and hearing impairments, we thank John J. Shields of the American Visionary Art Museum.

We are grateful for permission and the generously provided images from the Walters Art Museum, Smithsonian Museum of Asian Art – Freer Gallery of Art| Arthur M. Sackler Gallery, Tudor Place Historical Home and Garden, Smithsonian Museum of American Art, National Gallery of Art, and the University of British Columbia's Vancouver Museum of Anthropology. The Artists Rights Society granted licensing for the Rothko image.

Trudi Harkins generously copy edited the manuscript. Carol Macrini and Pat Morgan assisted with design and graphics.

Members of the National Docent Symposium Council reviewed the manuscript with care and made useful suggestions through all stages of its development.

Ordering Information

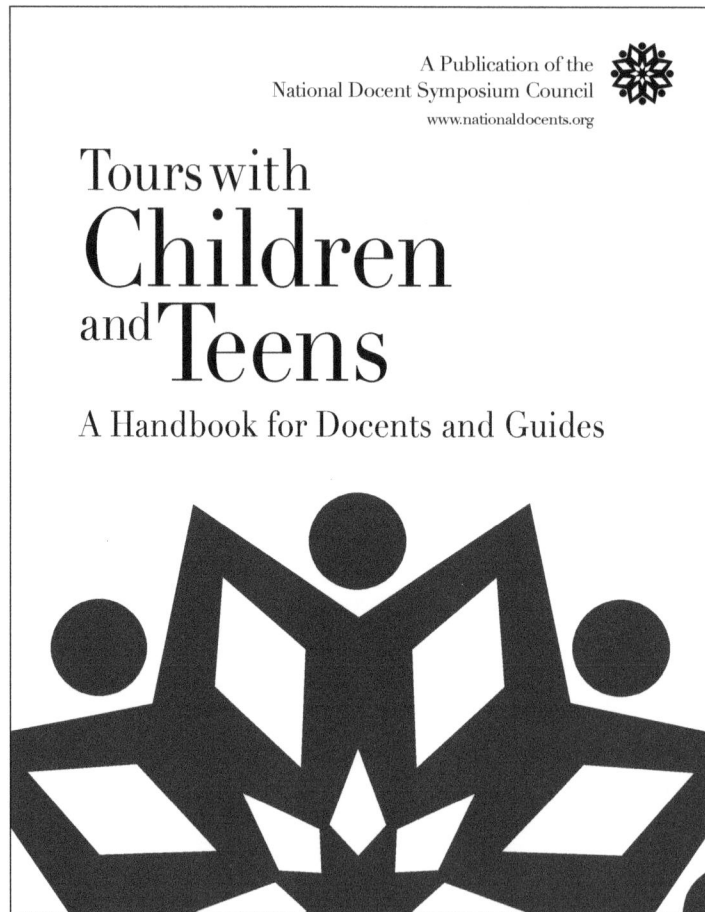

A Publication of the
National Docent Symposium Council
www.nationaldocents.org

Tours with Children and Teens

A Handbook for Docents and Guides

Sponsored by the National Docent Symposium Council

Please visit our website for current pricing
and direct order information.

www. nationaldocents.org